François Le Vaillant, Elizabeth Helme

Travels from the Cape of Good-Hope, into the Interior Parts of Africa

Vol. I

François Le Vaillant, Elizabeth Helme

Travels from the Cape of Good-Hope, into the Interior Parts of Africa
Vol. I

ISBN/EAN: 9783337124151

Printed in Europe, USA, Canada, Australia, Japan

Cover: Foto ©Andreas Hilbeck / pixelio.de

More available books at **www.hansebooks.com**

Designed and Engraved for
THE AFRICAN TRAVELS.

Dangerous Attack of a Tyger.

TRAVELS

FROM THE

CAPE of GOOD-HOPE,

INTO THE

INTERIOR PARTS OF AFRICA,

INCLUDING MANY

INTERESTING ANECDOTES.

WITH ELEGANT PLATES,

Descriptive of the Country and Inhabitants:

INSCRIBED BY PERMISSION TO

HIS GRACE THE DUKE OF MONTAGU.

TRANSLATED FROM THE FRENCH OF

MONSIEUR VAILLANT.

IN TWO VOLUMES.

VOL. I.

LONDON:

PRINTED FOR WILLIAM LANE, LEADENHALL-STREET.

M DCC XC.

TO HIS GRACE THE
DUKE OF MONTAGU,
MASTER OF THE HORSE TO THE
KING,
GOVERNOR AND CAPTAIN

OF

WINDSOR CASTLE,

LORD LIEUTENANT

OF THE

COUNTY OF HUNTINGDON,

ONE OF HIS MAJESTY'S

MOST HONOURABLE PRIVY COUNCIL,

KNIGHT OF THE MOST NOBLE

ORDER OF THE GARTER,

AND FELLOW OF THE ROYAL SOCIETY.

MAY IT PLEASE YOUR GRACE,

IMPRESSED with the sincereſt gratitude for the many favors received, permit me to return my most

most humble acknowledgments, and at the same time avail myself of your GRACE's permission, to present a translation of Monf. VAILLANT's Travels. Conscious that if, on inspection, he should be found faulty in other respects, his fondness for science, and love of humanity, will sufficiently recommend him to your GRACE, in whom those characters so conspicuously unite.

I am well aware, that your GRACE's judgment will discover many imperfections; an idea that would give me pain, were I not assured, that your GRACE's goodness is even superior to your high rank.

Should Monſ. Vaillant succeed in amusing an hour of your Grace's leisure, I shall deem the time passed in the translation amongst the most fortunate of my life.

I am, my Lord,
 With the utmost respect,
  Your Grace's
  Obliged, humble, and
  Most obedient Servant.

ELIZABETH HELME.

London, April 12th,
1790.

PREFACE

BY THE

TRANSLATOR.

AS there is a prefatory matter prefixed to the Work of Monf. VAILLANT, I fhould think it unneceffary to preface the Tranflation, did I not conceive it right to offer a few words of apology for a liberty I thought myfelf obliged to take, in fome places, with the Author; I mean, curtailing a few repetitions.

I have done this the more willingly, from an affurance that nothing has been expunged that could be either an aid to Science, inform the Naturalift, or even gratify a laudible curiofity.

I have likewise foftened (if I may be allowed the expreffion) a few paffages that poffibly might be accounted mere effufions of fancy and vivacity in a French author, but which would ill accord with the delicacy of a female tranflator, or indeed with the temper and genius of Englifh readers, with whom Monf. VAILLANT, notwithftanding, bids fair to become a great favorite, as he unites a daring fpirit of enterprize with another truly Britifh Characteriftic, namely Humanity.

As works of this kind are ufually divided into chapters, I thought it would be moft agreeable and convenient to the reader to adopt the ufual mode; the titles, therefore, of each chapter, fhould be confidered as the Tranflator fpeaking of the Author or his journey.

BY

MONSIEUR VAILLANT.

THAT part of Guiana, under the Government of the Dutch West-India Company, is perhaps the least known to naturalists, though it is without dispute (of all South America) the spot that offers the greatest variety of curious productions. Placed under the burning climate of the torrid zone, five degrees North of the line, this region, yet enveloped in the mist of time, conceals (if I may so express it) the focus where nature forces her exceptions to general rules. It has to an extent of an hundred leagues of Coaſt, a depth almoſt unlimited. Here the river of Surinam rolls its majeſtic courſe. On the left ſhore, three leagues from the ſea, ſtands Paramaribo, the capital of this vaſt Colony, which is my native country, the cradle of my infancy. Educated by inſtructed parents, who laboured to procure themſelves the intereſting and precious objects that enrich this region, I had continually under my eyes their acquiſitions, and enjoyed at eaſe the contemplation of a valuable cabinet, of which I ſhall hereafter have occaſion to ſpeak.

In my moſt early youth, my parents, who could not live without me, (though often undertaking tedious journeys to the fartheſt part of the colony) took me with them: Thus then my firſt ſteps were in the deſert, and I was almoſt born a ſavage. When reaſon (which ever exceeds age in hot climates)

climates) began to dawn, my inclinations were presently developed, and my parents aided to their utmost these first indications of curiosity. Under such good preceptors I daily enjoyed fresh pleasures; they held dissertations suited to the level of my comprehension, on objects they had procured, or hoped to procure: a confusion of ideas at first perplexed me, which were by little and little reduced to order; thus nature, to whom all my studies pointed, deigned to be my first instructor.

Soon a desire of imitation, the favorite passion of infancy, gave impetuosity, I might say impatience to my amusements; flattered by self-love, I imagined I likewise ought to have a cabinet of Natural History, and without loss of time declared war against Caterpillars, Butterflies, *Scarabees* (a species of Beetles) and in a word, all sorts of insects.

When we labour, even on our own account, 'tis poffible, by contracted means, with fmall fkill and application, to make little progrefs; but I think thofe generally fucceed who have neglected neither time, care, or trouble; thofe difpofitions being almoft certan to infure fuccefs. Every day I faw my collection of infects accumulate, which I valued beyond meafure, as they were all of my own procuring.

Thus far all was enjoyment, I had not yet felt the obftacles that prefent themfelves between enterprife and fuccefs.

In one of our excurfions we had killed a Monkey, of the kind called in this country *Baboon*, it was a female, and carried a young one on her back, which was not wounded; we took them both up, and on our return to the plantation, the young one had not yet left the back of its mother.

ther, holding so fast that I was obliged to get the assistance of a negro to separate them, which we had no sooner affected, than, with the swiftness of a bird, it darted to a block, on which was a wig of my father's, and clinging round it appeared satisfied; I therefore let him continue, feeding him with goat's milk. He remained in this situation for three weeks when he abandoned his nurse, and became by his tricks and merry conceits the friend of the family.

I had without suspicion placed the wolf in the sheep-fold, for one morning as I entered my apartment, the door of which I had imprudently left open, I saw my unworthy pupil breakfasting on my superb collection: In my first transports of fury I could have strangled him, but rage soon gave place to pity, when I saw how dreadfully he was punished for his gluttony, having, in cracking the Scarabees, swallowed

lowed the pins on which they were ſtuck. His torments made me forget his fault, and I only thought of giving him ſuccour, but my tears and all the art of the ſlaves could not ſave him from death. This accident threw me conſiderably back, but did not entirely diſcourage. I ſought new diſcoveries, and not content with one treaſure, wiſhed to re-unite ſeveral. By a natural progreſſion I now thought of birds, the ſlaves did not procure them to my liking, I therefore armed myſelf with a *Sarbacane*, (a tube to ſhoot with) and an Indian bow, which in ſome time I uſed with great ſkill, laying wait for whole days, it was now my former taſte become a paſſion, that diſturbed even my hours of reſt, and which time daily ſtrengthened.

Some friends have accuſed me of coldneſs and inſenſibility; a greater number have found the travels I have undertaken raſh, but I readily forgive the firſt, and have

have nothing to say for the latter. Yet if they deign to glance an eye on the first pursuits of my infancy, this appearance of originality will occasion less surprise, when they find my education at once the cause and the excuse.

Some time after my parents, who had fixed their departure for Europe, anxious to be re-united to their relatives, having settled their affairs, embarked, attended by me, on board the Catharina; on the 4th of April, 1763, we weighed anchor and sailed for Holland. In the joy of my heart I partook of all the pleasure and projects of my parents, during the voyage, a curiosity natural to my age, added to my transports; but this agitation, or rather delirium, did not render me insensible of regret, I could not so soon become ungrateful, my eyes were often cast back to the country where I received my being, to the shores which gradually lessened to my sight,

sight, and as I approached the frozen climates of the North, a profound melancholy overwhelmed me, preyed upon my soul and dissipated the promised enjoyments of the future. After a dangerous voyage we cast anchor in the Texel, at nine or ten o'clock in the morning of the twelfth of July following.

Arrived in Europe, all I beheld was new to me; I shewed so much impatience, fatiguing every one with questions, all appeared so extraordinary, that I, myself, was an object of astonishment to all that surrounded me; notwithstanding, my importunity did not always give the laugh against me, for I paid amply, in keen remarks on America, the information I gained of Europe.

After some stay in Holland, we went to a city in France, where my father was born; I was now in the bosom of my family,

family, and my inclinations had full scope for gratification, in the cabinet of Monf. de Becoeur; who, for the Ornithology of Europe, had the beft and moft numerous collection I have ever feen.

At Surinam I had a manner of fkinning birds which anfwered well enough, but fpoke little to the imagination, and yet lefs to the fight; I knew no method then of preferving the fkins, but placing them in large books: Here a new idea prefented; as well as preferving, I could make them retain their natural forms.— I determined to ftudy this art particularly, and became a keen fportfman.

During a ftay of two years in Germany, and feven in Lorraine and Alface, I made prodigious havock among the birds. I was alfo willing to be acquainted with their manners, and the diftinction of their various fpecies; and have often paffed
whole

whole weeks in watching, to procure myself a pair.

Thus then, in the space of eight or nine years, by care, trouble, and numberless attempts, I at length arrived at the art, not only of preserving these frail delicate creatures in their natural forms, but in that pure uninjured state, which constitutes the merit of my collection.

From long living among them, in fields, woods, and their most concealed retreats, I learned to distinguish the sexes in the most invariable manner, which though I do not consider as a very eminent merit, is the appendage of but a small number of Ornithologists. How often does it happen, that we see in very fine, and otherwise curious cabinets, forced divorces, and monstrous and unnatural alliances; in another place are classed, as male and female, two creatures who were never formed to meet;

and

and a little further, a male and female, of the same species, are announced as different kinds. I gathered more and more information in this part of Natural History, which was far from contenting me; I wished to act on a larger scale, when occasion seemed to call, and bid me defer it no longer.

In the Courant of 1777, a favourable circumstance conducted me to Paris; like all other strangers that arrive, for the first time, in that capital, I carried my tribute of admiration to the cabinet of the learned and curious. I was dazzled and enchanted with the beauty, variety of forms, richness of colours, and the prodigious quantity of every species, which, by forced contribution, came from all quarters of the world, and are classed, methodically, in a space, unhappily, ever too limited.

During

During three years residence, I saw and studied all the important cabinets at this place; these superb sights made me dissatisfied, and left a void in my heart. I saw this mass of foreign spoil, but as a general deposit, where the different beings were ranged without taste or choice; giving no information to science, and without any certain indication of their manners or affections. It was the study which in my earliest youth had most interested me; 'tis true, I knew several works on Natural History, but these were filled with palpable contradictions. I had read, with avidity, the immortal master-piece, consecrated to posterity by a great genius; I daily offered incense at his shrine; but his magic eloquence did not seduce me far enough to admire the flights of his imagination; nor can I pardon in the philosopher the exaggerations of the poet.

Above

Above all, I thought particularly, that those parts of the globe which were unexplored, might give new information, and rectify the former errors; looking on that man as supremely happy, who should have the courage to trace them to their source. The interior parts of Africa appeared, for that purpose, a Peru.——It was a virgin land.

Ingrossed with these ideas, I persuaded myself, that the ardour of zeal might supply genius. Enthusiasm whispered, I was the being for whom this privilege was reserved; I listened to the pleasing seduction, from which moment I became devoted; neither the ties of love or friendship were able to shake my purpose.——I communicated my projects to no one; but inexorable and blind to every obstacle, left Paris the 17th of July, 1780.

DIRECTIONS FOR PLACING THE PLATES.

VOL. I.

Dangerous Attack of a Tyger—Frontispiece	Facing Page.
View of the Cape of Good-Hope	16
View of the Camp, at Pampoen-Kraal	196
Klaas, the Author's favorite Hottentot	253
Ragel, a female Hottentot	309
Narina, a young Gonaquais	428

VOL. II.

Encampment among the Great Namaquais—Frontispiece	
Gonaquais Hottentot	2
Female Hottentot	50
Caffree	208
Female Caffree	263
Male and Female Girafe	456

TRAVELS
INTO THE
INTERIOR PARTS
OF
AFRICA.

CHAP. I.

THE AUTHOR LEAVES FRANCE——VISITS AMSTERDAM—EMBARKS FOR THE CAPE OF GOOD-HOPE—ACCOUNT OF AN ENGAGEMENT AT SEA—ARRIVES AT THE CAPE.

IMPATIENT to realize my project, I visited Holland, surveyed the principal cities of that famous republic, and their curiosities; Amsterdam contained treasures which even surpassed my idea. I was received with great kindness by the learned

learned men of that city, and permitted to inspect their cabinets: that which I most admired belonged to Minheer Temminck, treasurer to the India Company. Among his elegant collection, I noticed many things which I had never seen in France, and in the finest preservation. His superb aviary particularly, presented to the view, art and nature in combination to triumph over the climate. Here the eye was enchanted with admiration to behold, living, the most beautiful and rare birds, which by the cares bestowed on them build, breed and thrive as in their native country. This sight redoubled my former ardour, and determined me more than ever to conquer all obstacles and dangers that might obstruct my favorite design. M. Temminck honored me with distinguished friendship, it was particularly in his power to favor my intentions, these I had communicated to him, and he so much approved of them, that by his unwearied atten-

attention and kindnefs, I obtained leave to go to the Cape in a fhip belonging to the company.

From my truly refpected friend, I alfo received warm and generous recommendations, without which (as will be feen hereafter) I muft have been cruelly embarraffed.

Having procured neceffaries for fo long a voyage, and likewife what would be ufeful in the interior parts of Africa, I took leave of my friends and Europe, and was by a Shallop conveyed on board the *Held Woltemaade*, lying in the Texel, bound to Ceylon, and alfo to touch at the Cape. The Captain was called S——— V———. The wind proving contrary for our leaving the Texel, created a delay of eight days; during which time I learned that our fhip was fo named by the India Company, in memory of a glorious action
per-

performed by an inhabitant of the Cape, named *Woltemaade*, who during a dreadful storm, with only the assistance of his horse, saved the lives of fourteen sailors that were shipwrecked in Table Bay; but was at length the victim of his own generous efforts, himself and horse in the last attempt perishing from fatigue and weariness, together with the pressure of the remainder of the unfortunate crew, who were fearful of his return to save them before the vessel went to pieces. Of this melancholy catastrophe, there is a particular description in Dr. Sparman's Voyage to the Cape.

The wind changing, we weighed anchor on the 19th December, 1780, at eleven in the morning, being the day before the declaration of war between England and Holland; had it happened twenty-four hours sooner, we had not been permitted to depart: how unfortunate should I then have

have been, all my plans broken, all my hopes void.

Tempestuous weather, and a thick fog, enabled us to pass the Channel without being perceived by the English; having gained the open sea, we sailed with the greatest security, fearless of danger, because unknowing that the fury of war raged. We continued following our consort, the Mercury, with whom we sailed from the Texel, and under whose command we were, without any remarkable occurrence for some time, but we were soon to experience a change.

As I had foreseen that in a voyage of four, or perhaps six months, I might expect some heavy time, I provided myself with a few books; among those on natural history and voyages, was one by *La Caille*, which at first much amused me, but one day meeting with a passage Anti-Philanthropic, and full of fanatifm. I threw away my book, and determined to read no further; this is the paſſage: "The cuſtom of chaſing fugitive "negroes like brute beaſts, has nothing "in it that ſhould ſhock European ſenſi- "bility; for the moment men who ſhould "be uſeful members of the community, "from a ſpirit of libertiniſm and cupidity, "become the peſts of ſociety; they de- "grade themſelves below beaſts, and de- "ſerve the moſt rigorous chaſtiſement." But afterwards reflecting on the humane, kind and tolerant character which is ſo univerſally beſtowed on this learned writer, I retook my book, and found the following reflections. "But prejudice apart, "ſhould we prefer him who cultivates "the arts, and invents exceptions con- "trary to the rules and laws of nature; "or he who content with the moſt ſim- "ple, yet uſeful neceſſaries, follows the "maxims of ſtrict and ſcrupulous equity?" I now recollected that learning and ſcience

had

had been the ruin of *L'Abbe de la Caille*, before he had finished his journal, and deplored the ignorance of the editor in suffering a paragraph to appear which could never, in any manner, have escaped the pen of a priest, a philosopher, and a learned writer.

On the first of February, 1781, being three degrees North of the line, at break of day, we descried a sail in the horizon. It was a dead calm, and the Mercury almost out of sight. About nine, we could distinguish by the aid of our glasses a small vessel, which some thought French, others English, each forming different conjectures, reasoning in his own peculiar stile, and waiting for more certain information. We perceived some hours after, that it was towed by two shallops, and advanced fast towards us by the aid of oars: we now concluded it was a ship in distress coming to entreat our affiftance, and therefore let it advance without any hoftile preparation. At three in the afternoon being within half gun fhot, we hoifted our colours, and fired a gun with powder only: we were much furprifed to receive in return a ball in our ftern, which was followed by a broadfide; the privateer, at the fame time, hoifting Englifh colours.

It would be a vain attempt to paint the aftonifhment and ftupefaction that our whole crew were thrown into by this unforefeen adventure; there was not in our fhip a fingle man who had ever feen an action; the Captain and his officers had been ufed to voyage peaceably, confequently they had never commanded on a like occafion: thus attacked, fo unexpectedly, without time for preparation, or even to barricade the fhip, horror and confternation was painted on the features of our men; the officers

officers bawling, the soldiers all raw recruits, that perhaps had never fired a gun; in short, no one answering, or understanding a command. At seven we had not primed a gun; the privateer continued to cannonade, and threatened to sink us if we delayed striking; our Captain almost convulsed with fear, exclaimed, it was not in his power to surrender without leave from the Captain of the Mercury, who was his Commodore; indeed the poor fellow's head was absolutely turned.

At length, as if by miracle, the wind freshened, and the Mercury drew near enough to hail our Captain, and demand why he had not fired? his answer was, he waited for orders, that it was ever the commander who gave the signal to engage. A laughable excuse this in the mouth of a sailor, attacked by a small vessel with only sixteen eight pounders, while he had thirty-two of heavier metal, besides fides pattereroes, three hundred men, and plenty of ammunition. The Mercury engaging the enemy, we likewife followed her example, nowithftanding fhe was between us and the Englifh veffel, no matter! we now fired away—the confufion was favorable to our people, who tried to emulate each other—in drunkennefs, running backward and forward without knowing where, fome reeling and hollowing, others crying or fwearing, the reft hiding themfelves, even the chaplain (no doubt to infpire himfelf with courage) was guilty of the fame excefs; I faw him, with a lanthorn in his hand, going down to the powder room (which contained twenty-five thoufand weight of powder, deftined for Ceylon) and return, bringing without the leaft precaution, powder for cartridges; for, as I before obferved, there had not been the leaft preparation made previous to the engagement, although we had fo much warning.

We

We were abandoned by the enemy about eleven at night, and though they were foon at a diftance, we ftill kept firing.—What a glorious moment for cowards!—who now walked the deck with firm ftep, talking loud, and daring their opponents, long fince out of hearing. Notwithftanding this, fear was ftill predominant, no one daring to go to bed; like the reft, I paffed the night in the open air, ftretched on a fack, amidft a range of guns, every moment awaked by the vigilance of our watch, in whofe affrighted ears, the Englifh cannon ftill founded.

To give fome idea of the diforder that reigned during our late action, it may be only neceffary to add, that on an examination of the guns the day following, fome were found filled to the mouth, containing even three charges of powder thrown on each other, and as many balls; feveral guns were charged firft with bullets; in fine,

fine, had it not been for the Mercury, we had infallibly been taken; fortunately we were quit for a horrid fright only, for certainly nothing but fear could occasion such consternation among our officers, as to cause them to bear the cannonading of the enemy for four hours, without daring to risk a single fire. The English certainly thought we had no cannon, or that those they could not help observing were made of wood; for the least resistance on our part, must have made them give up the contest, and retire faster then they came.

I cannot finish this picture (truly worthy the sportive pencil of *Calot*) without mentioning a trait, that even at the time I write, forces me to smile; having no command in the ship, consequently no orders to give or receive during the fight; in the way to my cabin, I perceived the guardian of the company's papers faithfully seated by the mysterious box, ready to throw it into

into the sea on the least appearance of imminent danger. This man at least kept his post, but duty did not fix him there strongly as terror, which had almost mastered every other sensation. " Vaillant!" exclaimed he, " Vaillant! it is all over with " us, alas my friend we are undone, we " are lost." I used my utmost efforts to encourage and engage him, at least not to appear so visibly alarmed; when, lo! at this moment, a ball rushed through the cabin with a horrid crash, with a groan equally terrific, down dropt my man, without sense or motion; at first I really thought him dead, but after a short time he rose from the ground, weeping and sobbing. This sorrowful scene was too much for me, and I was obliged to quit the cabin to hide the laughter I could not suppress.

How ridiculous must this dastardly conduct appear in men, whose situation, age and

and experience, should rather render them examples of honour and bravery; more especially when we reflect that a little exertion would have dissipated all danger, and reduced to nothing so weak an enemy: their behaviour as men seemed to me still more pitiful, on reflecting that even boys, on similar occasions (though scarcely able to hold a cable) have given frequent instances of zeal, courage and intrepidity; nay, what was yet more disgusting, though at the same time somewhat diverting, the day after they seemed thoroughly convinced that the English ship must have sunk in consequence of their terrible cannonade; and the compliments the officers paid each other on the score of courage, were truly laughable. As I was well convinced the English had not received a single shot of ours, I could not help joking them, and communicated my thoughts on this business to the first pilot, *Van Groenon*, whom I had observed to behave

have as daſtardly as the beſt during the action, and who now gave himſelf as many airs of courage and prowefs. The common ſailors laughed in their ſleeves, it was not loſt on *Van Groenon*, who, however, put as good a face as poſſible on the matter, and contented himſelf with his own approbation, and that of his brother braggarts; to crown the work our Dr. Engelbreght, who during the action had hid himſelf in the bottom of the hold, was ordered to draw up an account of this glorious engagement. I took the liberty to rally the writer, as I had done the reſt; I did not fear his revenge, as I had the happineſs to enjoy a good ſtate of health. As for the pilot, he revenged himſelf for my jeſts, by making the voyage as diſagreeable as he could, but this I little regarded, as it was not to be of long duration; for excluſive of the *puiſſant ſea fight*, our voyage was fortunate, the wind continuing ſo favorable, that in three months and
ten

ten days from our departure, we discovered the mountains at the Cape, and the weather being clear and fine, I took a sketch of the shore and road as they first presented themselves to my view.

CHAP.

View of the

ten days from our departure, we discovered the mountains at the Cape, and the weather being clear and fine, I took a sketch of the shore and road as they first presented themselves to my view.

CHAP.

View of the Cape of Good-Hope.

CHAP. II.

DESCRIPTION OF THE CAPE, AND ITS INHABITANTS, WITH AN ACCOUNT OF THE SOUTH-EAST WIND THERE, &c.

WE anchored the same day in Table Bay; soon after which *Le Capitaine de Port* Minheer *Staring* came on board; he informed us of the declaration of war, which news had been brought them by a French frigate. The next day I landed, being impatient to pay my respects to those to whom my letters recommended me. I was received with distinguished

guished politeness; M. Boers, Fiscal, and M. Hacker, treated me with every mark of friendship and esteem; I felt that I did not owe this to superficial ceremony and complimentary grimace, which is too commonly made use of instead of the open and generous pleasure of serving our fellow creatures, and in reality, is only a perfidious art, the more securely to deceive a credulous stranger. They offered me all the services that my recommendations, or their distinguished rank could procure; I trusted to their honor, they were Hollanders, and scorned to deceive me.

I was impatient to explore this new country, whither I seemed transported as in a dream, every thing to my idea wore a pleasing aspect, and my eyes already wandered over the vast desert, which I was about to explore.

The

The town of the Cape is situated on the declivity of the Table and Lyon mountains, which form a natural amphitheatre that reaches to the sea; the streets though wide are not commodious, being ill paved; the houses, almost all built uniform, are spacious and handsome, the tops covered with reed, as heavier roofs might occasion accidents during the high winds. The inside contains no frivolous luxuries; the furniture is simple, yet neat and handsome; they use no hangings; pictures, and looking glasses are the principal ornaments.

On entering the town by the way of the Castle, the eye is presented with a number of elegant buildings. On one side the whole length of the gardens belonging to the Company. On the other, the fountains, whose waters descend from Table-Mountain by a channel, which may be seen from the town, and every part of the road. This water is excellent, and abun-

dantly

dantly supplies the inhabitants, as well as the vessels that touch at the Cape.

In general the men appeared well made, the women charming; I was surprized to see the stile in which they dressed, with all the minuteness and elegance of the French ladies; but they have neither their air or grace. As it is ever the slaves who suckle the children, a familiarity ensues that is highly prejudicial to their future manners and education; the latter, in men, seems in general still more neglected, if we except those who are sent to Europe for that purpose, there being no masters at the Cape, but those who teach writing.

The women in general play on the harpsichord; they likewise love singing, and are distractedly fond of dancing, so that a week seldom passes without their having several balls; the officers belonging to the ships in the Road, frequently
pro-

procure them this amusement. At my arrival, the governor had a custom of giving a public ball once a month, and the people of distinction in the town followed his example.

In a colony where so many strangers are continually arriving, I was astonished to find neither coffee-house nor tavern; but the truth is, every private house answers that purpose. The usual price for board and lodging is a piastre a day, (four and sixpence English) which is sufficiently dear, if we consider the scarcity of money in this country. While I was there butchers meat was very cheap; I have seen thirteen pounds of mutton bought for an escalin; (eleven-pence English) an ox for 12 or 15 rix dollars; (at six shillings and nine-pence English, the rix dollar) ten quarters of corn for 14 or 15 Rix-dollars, and other things in proportion. It is true that during the war, every thing was raised

raised to an extraordinary price, and toword the end of it, they gave 45 Rix-dollars for a sack of miserable potatoes; notwithstanding this enormous rise, the usual price of bcard was not advanced. Fish is very plenty at the Cape, among those in greatest estimation, they distinguish the *rooman*, a red fish found in False Bay; the *klepvis*, which is without scales, and taken among the rocks on the sea shore; the *steenbraasen*, the *stompneus*, and some others; but I should observe that these excellent ones only make their appearance at polite tables. Oysters are very scarce, they are only found in False Bay; eels are still scarcer, and I never saw any lobsters.

One must go several miles from the Cape to procure any game, those most common are the *steenbock*, the *duyker*, the *reebock*, the *grysbock*, and the *bontebock*; these are all different species of Gazells, (of which I shall speak more fully in my
de-

description of the quadrupeds) the hares, particularly that small kind which they call *lièvre de dune,* or down hare, are very numerous.

There are likewise several sorts of partridges, some large, others small; some more delicious than ours, others less so; the quail and woodcock differ not from those of Europe. They are only seen there during their passage.

Whatever the enthusiasts of the Cape may say, it seems to me that the European fruits have much degenerated there, I saw nothing I thought delicious except the grape. Cherries are both scarce and bad; pears and apples not much better, and will not keep; to balance this, the citrons and oranges (especially the sort called *naretyes*) are excellent; the figs delicate and wholesome, but the small banana, (otherwise called the pisan) is ill tasted. Is it not surprising

prising that so fine a country, under so pure a sky, (if we except some insipid berries) should produce no fruits natives of the soil? Neither asparagus nor artichoke grows at the Cape, but all other European vegetables seem naturalized, and are gathered all the year, if the south-east wind (which blows during three months) does not dry the earth in such a manner as to render it incapable of all kind of culture. This wind rages with such fury, that in order to preserve the plants, they are obliged to make a fence of hornbeam, round each division of the garden. They take the same care of the young trees, but notwithstanding all their precaution, they never put out branches on the side next the wind, and always incline in an opposite direction, which gives them a very disagreable appearance; in general it is very difficult to rear them.

I have

I have often been witnefs of the ravages made by this wind. In the fpace of twenty-four hours, the beft cultivated gardens are fometimes laid wafte; it rages moft from January to April, about the Cape, and much earlier up the country. In the courfe of my travels, my waggons were feveral times overfet by it, and I frequently had no means to prevent this, but by faftening them to trees. This wind announces itfelf at the Cape by a fmall white cloud, which at firft refts on the top of Table Mountain, on that fide next the Devil Mountain, the air foon begins to frefhen; by degrees the cloud augments, enlarging in fuch a manner that the whole fummit appears covered; at this time they ufually fay, *" the mountain has put on " its perriwig;"* it now finks rapidly; and hovering over the town, feems to threaten it with an immediate deluge; as it approaches the foot of the mountain, it begins to difappear, to evaporate and re-
duce

duce itfelf to nothing, but continues uninterruptedly calm and ... the mountain alone appears in the fog, which fhrouds it from the radiance of the fun.

I have often paffed the whole morning in examining this phenomenon without being able to comprehend the caufe; but after I had frequented Falfe Bay, on the other fide of the mountain, I have often taken pleafure in obferving the beginning and progrefs of it. The wind at firft blows very feebly, gently driving before it a fort of mift, which feems to detach itfelf from the furface of the fea; this mift collects, and preffed together by means of the obftacle it finds in its paffage on the South fide of Table mountain, not being able to free itfelf, heaps up by degrees, till it is elevated to the fummit; it then exhibits to the town that fmall white cloud which announces the wind, which in fact, has begun to blow fome hours

hours before on the sides of the mountain, in the road, and parts adj... The general duration of this kind of storm is three days succeffively, sometimes it continues without intermiffion much longer; it often likewise ceafes all at once, the atmofphere then becomes extremely fultry; and, if during three months (the time it ufually prevails) it fhould happen in this manner to have feveral fudden intermiffions, it is a certain prognoftic of a great deal of ficknefs.

Though this wind is not abfolutely dangerous to fhipping, inftances are not wanting of its ill effects on feveral; and when it becomes too impetuous, it is prudent, in order to avoid an accident, to gain the open fea; when it does not bear the mifts, it only blows in the road, and is of no confequence in the town, for it is only a vaft collection of thefe fogs rufhing violently along that occafions thofe terrible hurricanes

canes which they sometimes experience, and which render it almost impossible to walk in the streets; and notwithstanding the exactitude and care, with which they shut their doors and windows, the dust at this time penetrates even into their cupboards and trunks. Whatever inconveniences may accompany it, this wind is of infinite service to the town, by purging it of those noxious vapours which arise from the filth that is naturally collected about the sea coast, from what the inhabitants throw out, but above all, from the offal exposed by the company's butchers, who neither make use of the heads, feet, nor entrails of the animals which they kill, leaving them in heaps at the doors of their slaughter houses, where they corrupt and impoison both the air and the inhabitants, fomenting those epidemical distempers which are but too common at the Cape, especially when the South East wind has not been very violent.

The most cruel and dangerous disease at this place is the sore throat. People of the most robust constitutions frequently fall victims to this malady in three or four days. It is a sudden and violent stroke which gives no warning.

The small-pox is another scourge to these colonies. This part of the globe was a stranger to it till the arrival of the Europeans; but since it has been under the dominion of the Dutch, this disorder has brought it to the very brink of destruction; particularly when it first made its appearance, it swept off more than two thirds of the Colonists.

Its ravages were still more dreadful among the Hottentots; it seemed as if this malady attacked them in preference to others, and even now they are extremely subject to it.

At

At prefent all veffels on their arrival in the road, are fcrupuloufly examined by the furgeons belonging to the company, and if they difcover the leaft veftige of this diforder, all communication with the inhabitants is moft rigoroufly forbidden; an imbargo is laid on the cargo, of which they will not fuffer the fmalleft article to be landed, and they keep day and night a very ftrict guard over them.

If it fhould be known that a Captain had concealed this malady on board his fhip, he and his officers would be degraded on the fpot, and condemned to pay a very heavy fine, if the veffel belonged to the company.

I have faid *his officers,* becaufe every one of them being accountable for the fhare of command he has on board, it would be impoffible to conceal the contagion without the unanimous confent of
the

the whole crew. If a foreign ſhip ſhould be in theſe circumſtances, nothing could poſſibly ſave it from confiſcation.

The rainy ſeaſon uſually commences about the end of April. It is more abundant and more frequent in the town than in its environs; the natural reaſon of which is, the North wind at the Cape has the ſame effect that the South-Weſt has in France; it brings a great number of clouds with it, which as they approach the town, are encountered and broken by the Table, Devil, and Lion mountains. At this time it rains without intermiſſion at the Cape, though at two leagues diſtance all round they enjoy a clear ſky and dry weather.

Sometimes the rain ſpreads over the whole ſpace between Table Bay, and Falſe Bay, to the Eaſt of that chain of enormous mountains which extend themſelves to the very point of Africa, while the Weſtern

Western side is clear and without a cloud.

This is a feeble image of what happens on the coasts of Coromandel and Malabar, except that here this spectacle is more wonderful, because, being nearer, it is more obvious.

Suppose two friends were to set off from the town at the same instant for False Bay, he that takes the East side of the mountain should carry his *paraplue*, while he that takes the West would have occasion for his *parasol:* they arrive at the place of rendezvous, the one fatigued with heat, and panting under the burning ray; the other frozen with cold, and dropping with rain.

Strangers are generally well received at the Cape by those who are in the service of the company, and by some other individuals,

duals, but the English are adored there; whether it is that there is some analogy in the manners of the two nations, or rather that they affect a great portion of generosity.

Thus much is certain, that the inhabitants of the Cape are eager to offer them their lodgings. In less than eight days every thing in the house is English; the master, mistress, and children, intirely adopting the manners of their inmates. At table for instance, they never fail to make the knife perform the office of the fork. Of all nations the French are the least esteemed here; the common people in particular cannot endure them. This hatred is carried to such a length, that I have frequently heard the inhabitants aver, they would rather have been taken by the English, than have owed their safety to the French arms. At that time I took these discourses for an exaggeration, and thought these people made light of command, in order to lessen the value of those services which France had actually rendered them, and in the same proportion the debt of gratitude due on that account. Whatever may have occasioned this, I believe the French would have found great reason to complain of this colony, had it not been for some leading people, whose prudence checked the murmurs of the multitude, while their obliging and essential services in every circumstance that could possibly occur, balanced in some measure this unjust and ungrateful dislike.

These worthy men are not unknown to the French minister, who has honored them with two letters of acknowledgment on the part of his sovereign: and who would not render his tribute of praise to the noble and disinterested conduct of M. *Boers*, fiscal, or forget to cherish the memory of

it

it in his heart? for my part, I render him the moſt pure and ſincere homage. May this truth that eſcapes me, while it pains his modeſty, ſpread as it ought, the knowledge and remembrance of his virtues!

CHAP. III.

DEPARTURE FOR AND DESCRIPTION OF SALDANHA BAY—VISITS SCHAAPEN AND MONKEY ISLANDS—THE CACHALOT DESCRIBED.

THE news of the rupture between England and Holland, which had reached the Cape before our arrival, with the aſſurances we gave that the Engliſh were

were not idle, made them entertain the liveliest apprehensions of a visit from the enemy; in consequence of which, the government judged it necessary to make some preparations, and that the vessels in the Road, and in Table Bay, should immediately take refuge in the bay of Saldanha, where they would stand some chance of escaping the researches of the English; and orders to this effect were dispatched to each of the Captains. This event seemed to favour the prosecution of my designs; accordingly I proposed departing with the fleet. M. *Vangenep*, who commanded the *Middelbourg*, had the complaisance to offer me a very agreeable accommodation on board his ship, with every facility to prosecute those researches which I had in meditation, when we should arrive at the bay. I accepted his offers of service, with feelings of the most lively gratitude, got my effects on board, and on the tenth of May we hoisted sail in company with four other

On the entrance of this bay, on the right hand fide, it indents itfelf in a diagonal direction for the fpace of feven or eight leagues; on the oppofite fide near the mouth, there is a fmall creek called *Hoetjis Bay*. Ten or twelve fail may find anchorage in this place on a good bottom: it is eafy for lighter veffels to go further up, to a little ifle, called *Schaapen Ifland*, where they are fheltered from all winds.

The water here is much inferior to that at the Cape, but during the monfoons, it changes its nature and becomes excellent. The country people bring all forts of provifions to the fhips which vifit this place at a much lower price than at the Cape town; fo that a fhip failing from Europe, and prevented by the South-Eaft winds from making Table Bay may gain that of *Saldanha,* and be sure of finding refreshments in abundance.

The Company maintains a trifling post at this place, consisting of a few men under the command of a corporal, who, when he perceives a ship at the mouth of the Bay, sends an express by land with advice of it to the governor at the Cape.

The *Cachalots* (a sort of whale, which the Dutch call *noord-kaaper*) are very numerous, and continually playing in this bay. I have frequently shot at them when they have raised themselves above the surface of the water, but it never seemed to have the least effect on them.

We found a prodigious quantity of rabbits on *Schaapen-Island*; it became our warren, and was an excellent resource for our crews. All sorts of game abound in its environs, especially the little gazells called

called *Steenbock*, with all those I have before specified. Partridges and hares are likewise met with here, but the difficulty of walking over this deep sandy coast, renders hunting very difficult and fatiguing. Panthers are very common, but they are not so fierce as in many other parts of Africa; because the game furnishing them with plenty of provision, they are not drove to extremities by hunger.

Some days after my arrival, the commander of the before-mentioned post invited me to hunt with him. The next day we actually set out. We saw plenty of game, but at such a distance that our shot would not reach them. Towards evening, by accident, I got seperated from my companion.

Chance now seemed resolved to familiarise me all at once, with the dangers I had come so far in search of. At a time when

when I had not the leaſt idea of it, I experienced them rather abruptly, and in a manner that might have made the braveſt tremble.

The report of my piece had ſtartled a young gazelle; I thought my dog was in queſt of it; he ſtopped at a large clump of buſhes, began to bark violently, and kept running perpetually round them. I made no doubt but the gazelle had taken refuge there, and haſted to the ſpot in hopes of killing it. My preſence and voice greatly encouraged my dog, and I expected every moment to ſee it make its appearance; tired with waiting, I entered myſelf among the buſhes, beating them on all ſides of me with my fowling piece, in order to facilitate my paſſage. It is impoſſible to expreſs the horror and ſurpriſe that froze me, when in the centre of the thicket, I encountered, face to face, an enormous and furious panther! His pan-

manner the moment he saw me—his eyes glaring—his neck extended—his mouth half open—his hollow growling, which seemed to announce my immediate destruction—I already thought myself devoured!

The intrepidity of my dog saved me; he kept the animal at bay, who seemed unable to decide between his fear and rage. I retired softly till I had gained the edge of the thicket; my faithful dog followed my example, and seemed resolved to perish with his master. I regained the open plain, and lost no time in recovering the post road, though not without frequently looking behind me; mean time, I heard at a distance, and at intervals, the report of a musket. I made no doubt but it proceeded from my companion, who was seeking me. It was night, and I had no inclination to join him. It was late before he returned. His surprise equalled

his

his joy on finding me safe and well. He had suppofed from hearing the barking of my dog, that I was attacked by fome tyger or hyæna, and as I did not anfwer his firing, concluded I was torn to pieces.

When I related my adventure, it occafioned a great deal of laughter; and from his account of what I fhould have done in this predicament, I regretted that I had not endeavoured to kill the animal; but I was unacquainted with countries infefted with wild beafts; this was the firft I had encountered, and I was totally ignorant in what manner I fhould have dealt with it. Thus I employed my leifure hours, and accuftomed myfelf infenfibly to the greateft dangers.

We often reforted to *Schaapen-Ifland* to fhoot rabbits. In one of thefe excurfions, (which till now had proved extremely

plea-

pleasant) we were in the most imminent danger; on a sudden a *Cachalot* raised itself up so near our shallop as to give us the greatest apprehensions for our safety, lest in falling it should overwhelm us with its enormous weight. Some of the sailors leaped over-board, but the man at the helm put about so opportunely that we avoided the danger. The monster reared itself at least twelve feet above the surface of the sea, and on replunging into the water, threw up such a quantity as wet us all over. Our shallop received so violent a shock that we were apprehensive of its sinking, and had it not been for the pilot's presence of mind, it is certain that none of us should have escaped death.

The *Cachalot* is ordinarily from sixty to eighty feet long, sometimes longer, and it frequently raises itself half its length out of the water, and when this heavy
mass

mass falls again it makes a noise like the sound of a cannon.

One night while we were at supper, our vessel had so extraordinary and convulsive a motion, that, not knowing what to think of it, we hastily quitted the table and ran to the deck; the alarm was general on board; *Vangenep* thought we had dragged our anchors, and drifted against a rock, but convinced by the situation of the other vessels, that we had not changed our position, he immediately gave up that idea. Our anxiety redoubled, and we eagerly sought the cause of this extraordinary motion, when we discovered a *Cachalot*, who at the moment rose a-head of us. He had doubtless entangled his tail (the fins of which spread to an amazing width) between our cables, which happened to be crossed, and in his furious efforts to disengage himself had violently shook, and yet continued to agitate the vessel.

fel. Our people jumped into the shallops, and got ready their harpoons, but unhappily the obscurity of the night retarded those manœuvres which were necessary for the taking of it, and before the shallops were ready it disengaged itself and made its escape. They were all disappointed, myself very much so, and I continued to regret it till chance threw another in my way, and gave me an opportunity of satisfying my curiosity.

The danger over, we replaced ourselves at table, and as false alarms usually create mirth, amused ourselves with bantering each other, and speaking ludicrously of the different impressions which fear had made on each.

The regularity and vigilance with which the orders of *Vangenep* were given on this occasion, was a certain indication that he conceived our situation to be extremely

dan-

dangerous; but his fears were not conspicuous; and it is certain that courage and coolness often mask dangers, and encourage the multitude. Such will ever be the conduct of a good officer. Consternation soon spreads itself, when once the men see dismay painted on the features of their Captain. I could not help reflecting on the difference between this scene and the former one, on my crossing the line, when we were so shamefully cannonaded. as before related.

In *Saldanha* Bay, there is a little isle called *Daſſen-Iſland*, or (the isle of monkies) I do not know whether those animals were formerly found there, but I never saw any of them. By common tradition, I learned that a Danish vessel being hindered by contrary winds from entering the road at the Cape, had taken shelter in this Bay; where, after some little stay the Captain died, and was buried

Every time I went to *Schaapen* island, as we approached this place, a kind of hollow found, which had fomething dreadful in it, ſtruck my ear. I ſpake of this to the Captain; he anſwered, that if I had the ſmalleſt inclination that way, we would pay it a viſit, for that he himſelf ſhould like to fee the Daniſh tomb. The next morning he gave orders accordingly, and we ſet off on this expedition.

In proportion, as we approached this place the noiſe excited our curioſity, the more ſo, as the ſea breaking with violence againſt the rocks (which form a kind of rampart round this iſland) ſeemed to re-echo the hollow buzzing, the cauſe of which we could not poſſibly divine. At length we arrived, I cannot ſay we landed, for the earth was covered with water, and

and the furf was fo violent that we were every moment covered with it.

With great difficulty and danger we climbed up the rocks and gained the level plain. Never did a more extraordinary fpectacle prefent itfelf to mortal eye! There arofe from the whole furface of the ifle, an impenetrable cloud which formed, at about forty or fifty feet above our heads, an immenfe canopy, or rather fky of birds of all forms, and of all colours: cormorants, fea-gulls, fwallows, pelicans, all the feathered inhabitants of the air who frequent this part of Africa, feemed affembled in this place; while all their various croakings mingled together, and modified according to their different kinds, formed mufic, that I was every moment obliged to ftop my ears in order to diminifh the din, and afford myfelf fome relaxation.

The

The alarm was the more general among thefe innumerable legions of birds, as we had principally to do with females; it was precifely the feafon of their breeding, and they had their nefts, their eggs, and young ones to defend. They attacked us like enraged harpies, and actually deafened us with their cries. Sometimes they fought on full wing, even rufhing with violence againft us; they feemed regardlefs of our fhot, and nothing was capable of difperfing them; nor could we make a ftep without crufhing either eggs or young ones under our feet. The earth was abfolutely covered with them.

The caverns and crevices of the rocks were inhabited by *Phocafes* and *Mors*, a fort of fea calves, and fea lions. We killed among others, one of the latter fort of an enormous fize.

The moſt trifling ſhelter furniſhes a retreat for the *manchots*, who abound above all others. This bird which is about two feet high, does not carry his body like other birds but walks perpendicularly on its feet, with a laughable air of gravity, and what renders its appearance ſtill more ridiculous, the wings, entirely devoid of feathers hang negligently by their ſides, and are of no uſe except in ſwimming. As we advanced towards the middle of the iſle, we encountered innumerable troops of them ſtalking along erect. Theſe creatures did not by any means derange themſelves on our appearance, but crowded particularly about the above mentioned monument in ſuch manner as ſeemed to forbid our approach; every avenue was obſtructed by them. Nature had added to the ſimple tomb of this poor Daniſh Captain, what the imagination of the poet, and the chiſſel of the artiſt could not poſſibly have reached. The beſt ſculptured

tured screech owl on our most superb mausoleum has not so hideous, so melancholy an aspect as the *manchot*: the mournful notes of this bird, mingled with the cries of the sea calf, impress the mind with sorrow, and form the heart to tenderness. For some time I fixed my eyes on this last asylum of an unfortunate voyager, and offered the tribute of a sigh to his manes.

A monument raised in haste could offer nothing in itself worthy the remarks of a curious traveller; it was a long square about three feet in height, composed of the broken pieces of rock which the surrounding isle afforded. I wished to see the inside of it; perhaps it contained, with the melancholy remains of the Captain, some account of his death, or of his family. Had I been alone I should certainly have explored it, but being with Dutch sailors, I did not dare to make the offer; they scrupulously respect the dead, and would have

have looked on me with horror and deteſtation had I attempted to diſturb this peaceful ſolitary tomb. They are ſuperſtitious to exceſs, and had any accident befallen the veſſel would not have failed placing it to that account, I therefore prudently concealed my deſires, but reſolved to gratify them at ſome future opportunity.

We loaded our ſhallop with the ſeveral ſorts of animals we had caught. The *Manchots* were not forgotten; they furniſhed us with a quantity of oil for our lamps; the ſailors had picked up a quantity of eggs, that ſerved us for ſeveral days; they were delicious, and ſeaſonably relieved the ſameneſs of our dry and common ſea proviſion: I ſhall add to this digreſſion (which I thought intereſting) a few words concerning the ſea lyon and calf. They are ſpoke of by authors differently, and their deſcriptions have ſo
claſhed

clashed with each other, that in the end, the readers have been compleatly bewildered; all I can say of the former of these monsters is, that I could never discover those trunks half a foot long, which we are persuaded to believe hang to the extremity of the upper jaw of the males. For the latter, which the Dutch have given this name to, it is the same that they shewed three or four years ago in the shops of the *palais royale*; and which they then called a *sea tiger*, at the same time in another place, they shewed one of the same kind under a different name, but all this is nothing to what follows, for the honest credulous Parisians, who fifteen years before would not have gone a step to see a camel, ran in crowds to view a *gangan*, which was nothing more than a camel new baptized by a rogue. Such impositions are more to be condemned than ridiculed; they propagate ignorance among

in-

indolent people: the sacrifice they make of their money to satisfy simple curiosity, ought at least to give them some instruction. We had hardly been three months in the Bay, yet I already was acquainted with all its environs, and had been so well employed about my principal object, as to be able to collect a considerable number of curious birds, shells, insects, plants, and marine productions; but alas! an unfortunate event soon deprived me of the fruits of my labour.

CHAP.

THE SHIPS IN SALDANHA BAY ATTACKED BY A SQUADRON UNDER COMMODORE JOHNSTONE—THE AUTHOR LOSES HIS EFFECTS—ASSISTS IN KILLING A PANTHER—RETURNS TO THE CAPE.

WE received an exprefs by land from the governor, which informed us that Monfieur de Suffrein, after the affair of St. Jago, was arrived at the Cape, where he daily expected to be joined by another French fleet; this exprefs also brought orders for the *Held Woltemaade*, (the fhip in which I came

came from Europe) to depart immediately for Ceylon, the place of its destination. Poor Captain S—— V—— failed the beginning of August, this fatal ship had followed us to *Saldanha Bay*, and it certainly was written in the book of fate that it should not depart until it had compleated my ruin.

When I reflected on our ridiculous combat with the privateer, I could not but think the *Held Woltemaade* would be taken as soon as perceived by the English, and so it happened; for hardly had it set sail, before it was taken, and manned by the squadron of Commodore Johnstone; this caused the misfortune, the English being informed of our situation by the indiscretion of the crew, presented themselves at the mouth of the Bay, and hoisted French colours, we believed it to be the fleet of our allies which we daily expected, but were soon undeceived by a cutter a-head

of

of the reft, hoifting the Englifh flag, and firing a broadfide, which was followed by the reft of the fleet; the force was too great to admit of a difpute, we therefore cut our cables and run aground, each feeking his fafety in flight; diforder and confufion inftantly reigned, and the unfortunate fhips were left to be ranfacked and plundered, every one taking what he could carry with him; our Captain fet fire to his fhip, the Englifh reached the reft time enough to prevent their undergoing the fame fate. The fear of being purfued and taken, made our failors haften on the road to the Cape; they had twenty leagues of land to crofs before they reached the town; this difcouraged feveral, who were fo loaded that they were obliged to leave part of their effects on the way, the different paths they had taken were ftrewed with them. Unhappily that day I was hunting, the noife of the cannon reached me, I naturally thought it fome re-

rejoicing aboard our squadron, and hastened to enjoy it; arriving on the Downs what a sight presented itself to my view! The Middleburgh at that moment blew up, covering the sea and air with flaming fragments thus in one instant I had the misfortune to behold my effects, my project, my collection, and all my hopes dispersed in air, and vanished in smoke!

All this time the English kept cannonading the Downs, and capturing those whom covetousness had left in the ships; of five prisoners that we had on board, four had thrown themselves in the sea on the discovery of the English flag, and joined their countrymen; the fifth had prefered landing with us; he was on the Downs within ten paces of me, I knew him, and as well as I could in his own language was asking him a question respecting this horrid catastrophe; a bullet that took off his head, prevented his answer,

swer; another from the same broadside did as much for a great dog that appeared seeking his master, and had drawn near me scared and trembling. These two bullets made me dread a third, I therefore abandoned the spot that moment and went to shelter myself on the other side of the Downs.

What was my situation after this terrible adventure! it is not to be supposed I would go to the Cape, to ask pecuniary assistance and encrease the multitude of unhappy victims, who had escaped the fire or bonds of the enemy; as I was not particularly concerned in this scene of horror, I should have run no risk, for I could derive no benefit from it, without title, without command, alone, separated from every thing that was dear to me! These ideas, with the rapidity of lightening struck on my mind, and gave a shock to my very soul. Two thousand leagues from my wife,

wife, my children, and my adopted country, without friends, without shelter, almost without hope; my only resources were my gun, six ducats in my pocket, and the clothes I had on. What remained for me? What must become of me? tears now bedewed my cheeks. In this deplorable situation, directing my eyes to the shore, a disturbed imagination presented the conquerors pursuing the vanquished. Savage ferocity for the first time took possession of my heart, and for a moment I wished that a shot from the enemy would by ending my life spare me further misery.

But sorrow can go but one particular length, and my first gloom gradually subsiding, reflection comfortably assured me that despair should never overbalance hope, whilst youth and vigour afforded the means of exertion. It occurred to me that a Colonist I had often seen in hunting, and

(and who lived about four leagues off) would suffer me to remain with him, until I could receive supplies from my family in Europe; I repaired to this man's solitary dwelling, and entreated his affistance, misfortune had marked my features with diftrefs, the humane, generous *Slaber* received me with open arms, then took me by the hand, and prefented me to his family. From this time, I imitated the indefatigable fwallow, whofe neft has been cruelly deftroyed, like her I again fet to work, and began, though not without forrow, the foundation of another collection. Some days after we received news from the Cape that all the Captains (except Vangenep) were broke, he being the only one who had blown up his fhip, which though ruin to me, was a good action for his country, as it prevented her falling into the enemy's hands. On leaving the Cape, they had all received orders (if attacked beyond the power of defence) to fire

fire their ships, which previously were to be unrigged, and the cordage, sails, &c. put on board a *Hoeker* (a vessel that drew but little water) which was to anchor further up the Bay, close in shore as possible. The latter part of this order had been obeyed on the vessel's first arrival at Saldanha Bay, and had the Captain of the *Hoeker* fired her, as he had received orders to do, it would have greatly embarrassed the enemy, who in all probability must have been reduced to the necessity of leaving our ships behind them, as they could not have taken them away for want of rigging, or at the worst they must have blown them up as Captain *Vangenep* had done the Middleburgh. On the English cutter's approaching the Hoeker, her Captain landed with the utmost precipitation, and so far from firing his vessel, he had not even made the least preparation for that purpose, but instead of it, by an inconceivable spirit of contradiction, not to say

say madness, set on fire, and reduced to ashes, an elegant habitation at the extremity of the Bay, in a place where the water was so shallow that even shallops could not land; he was afterwards prosecuted by the proprietor *Le Sieur Heufke* for damages, who expected to recover the whole amount of his loss.

Vangenep was the only Captain on our arrival at Saldanha that had made the necessary preparation for executing punctually the orders given at the Cape, in consequence our vessel was stowed with faggots, and compleatly larded in every part with oiled tow, pitch, tar, and other combustibles. The other Captains were the less pardonable, as they had been three months in the Bay without employ: for we arrived the eleventh of May, and this affair happened the beginning of August.

The

The officers and sailors running tumultuously to the town, had but too much spread the news of our defeat.

M. Boers, Fiscal, not seeing me return, made so much enquiry, that he soon discovered the retreat I had chosen; in a few days he arrived, how much did I then regret my having been divided from so kind a friend. I gave him an account of the unhappy situation, to which the common misfortune had reduced me, by the loss of all I had possessed; I likewise informed him of my resolution to stay with the honest *Slaber*, until I had received news from my family, and assiduously endeavour in the mean time to regain a collection equal to my former, and extend my knowledge in natural history. M. Boers heard me out without the smallest interruption, would it were possible I could engrave in letters of gold his tender reproaches, and pressing solicitude, to go

with

with him even that minute; this proposal was made without haughtiness, or the consequential impatience that in general accompanies the offers of European protection, all was that open frankness, which ever judges of others by itself, and deems the obliged worthy the benefit. In answer to my excuses, " Sir," said he, " you
" must not forget you was recommended
" to me, the hour of your unhappiness is
" the time when I should shew myself wor-
" thy the confidence my friends repose.
" I will not deceive them, my house, my
" table, and every assistance in my power
" is at your service; take courage, make
" another effort, re-assume your researches,
" and do not let uncertain news from
" Europe prevent your travels; leave the
" resources to me, you shall not refuse.
" ——I will have it so."

His generous offer was conveyed with such honest warmth, that I plainly perceived

ceived a refusal would give him pain; I therefore accepted it, and to this worthy friend I owed the advantage to apply myself without more delay, for the desired journey, as well as the considerable expence that attended its execution: often do I read the remembrance of this kindness, it is engraven on my heart; with equal gratitude I reflect on the favors I received from Mr. Hacker, lieutenant governor, while at the Cape. To Mr. Gordon, commander of the troops, my thanks are likewise due for the services he rendered me; his curious observations published in Holland by Allaman, are much esteemed, and I must own that to them I am greatly obliged for a number of curious details of objects, which perhaps might have escaped me, had I not received instructions and council before my departure, from an author who had himself visited some parts of the country.

I asked

I asked permission to pass a fortnight at Saldanha, to repair if possible a small part of the loss I had sustained, not knowing whether I should have it in my power to return to this unfortunate spot.

At least I wished to furnish myself with particulars, which I was almost certain I could not procure elsewhere.

I was so perfectly acquainted with the spot, that I may say I had only to reach out my hand for them, for before the tragical history of our vessel, I had purchased a horse, and hired a Hottentot, to attend me, who had led me to the most unfrequented spots; my host and his two sons assisted, on the least sign they would have prevented my wishes; it might have been imagined they were at my command; never could I look at these honest people without astonishment and admiration.

The good *Slaber* had likewise three daughters of pleasing appearance, and fine forms, indeed none of the family measured less than six feet.

I employed in the best manner possible the fifteen days, I had with so much trouble obtained from my friends: shells, plants, and hunting, took up all my time, the last particularly was my favorite diversion, though it was perpetually exposing me to the greatest dangers, and I had gained a character for intrepidity ten leagues round.

One evening that I returned early, I found at our dwelling one of the inhabitants I was unacquainted with, he had been waiting for me, his name was *Smit*, he was come to solicit our assistance against a tyger, that had for some time infested his division, and carried away regularly every night some of his cattle; his entreaty

gave

gave me pleasure, I accepted it with joy, delighted to have a regular chace of that animal, and determined to revenge myself on this, for the fright I had before received from his fellow. We fixed on the next day, persuading some young men in the environs to accompany us; I remarked they did not much like the business; however, I contrived to shame the most fearful, and this served as a spur to the rest. We got together all the dogs we could find, and provided ourselves with arms. Thus every thing ready prepared for the assault, we separated until morning. I then went to bed, but could not close my eyes from impatience; at break of day I gained the plain with my escort (*Smit*, and some of his friends) we were in all eighteen, about the same number of dogs. *Smit* informed us the tyger had that night robbed him of a sheep. One of my guns was loaded with large pieces of lead, another with shot, and a carbine with balls, two of which my

Hot-

Hottentot carried as he followed me. The country was tolerably open, except here and there a few divided thickets, which we were obliged to beat with great precaution.

After an hours fruitless search we found the half devoured carcass of the sheep, this assured us the animal was not far off, and could not escape. Some few moments after our dogs, who till that time had been beating confusedly about, pressed together, and rushed within two hundred paces of us into a large thicket, barking and howling as loud as possible.

I leaped from my horse, gave him to my Hottentot, and running to the side of the thicket, got on a rising ground within fifty paces; casting my eyes back I perceived my companions were alarmed. However, John Slaber, (son of my host) came up, saying he would not abandon me, though in danger of his life. By the

agitation

agitation of his appearance, and the fear which was marked on his countenance, I judged the poor lad gave himself up for loſt I well knew that the apparent firmneſs of another would encourage him, and indeed, though his terror was extreme, I believe he thought himſelf in greater ſecurity when near me, than in the midſt of his poltroon companions, who were gazing upon us at a reſpectful diſtance. I had been told that in caſe I ſhould be near enough to the animal to be heard, I muſt not ſay *ſaa, ſaa,* for that word would render the beaſt furious, and that he would ruſh on the perſon that uttered it; as I had company, I was not afraid of being ſurpriſed therefore repeated the word a hundred times together, by the way of encouraging the dogs, and likewiſe to drive the beaſt from the thicket ; but all in vain, the animal and dogs were equally fearful of each other, the former not daring to quit his retreat, nor the latter to enter it; yet among the maſtiffs there were ſome that muſt have ſucceeded had their courage equalled their ſtrength; my dog, the ſmalleſt of the pack, was always at their head, he alone advancing a little into the thicket. It is true, he knew me, and was animated by my voice. The hideous beaſt roared terribly, every moment I expected it to ruſh out, the dogs on its ſmalleſt motion, drew haſtily back, and ran as faſt as poſſible; at length a few random ſhot diſlodged him, and he ruſhed out ſuddenly: his appearance ſeemed the ſignal for every one to decamp, even John *Slaber* (formed with the ſtrength of a Hercules, able to wreſtle with the animal, and ſtrangle him in his arms) abandoned me, and ran to the others—I remained alone with my Hottentot. The panther in endeavouring to gain another thicket, paſſed within fifty paces of us, with all the dogs at his heels, we ſaluted him by firing three ſhot as he paſſed us.

The

The thicket in which he had taken refuge was neither so high, large, or bushy as the one he had quitted; a track of blood made me presume I had wounded him, and the fury of the dogs was a proof I was not mistaken; a number of my people now drew near, but the greater part had entirely disappeared.

The animal was baited more than an hour, we firing into the thicket more than forty random shot, at length (tired and impatient with this tedious business,) I remounted my horse, and turned with precaution on the opposite side to the dogs. I imagined that employed in defending himself against them, it would be easy to get behind him; I was not mistaken, I saw him squatting, and striking with his paws to keep at bay my dog that ran barking within the reach of his fangs. When I had taken the necessary steps to catch him in a good situation, I fired my carbine, this

I im-

I immediately dropped to catch up my gun, which I carried at the bow of my faddle; this precaution was ufelefs, the animal did not appear, nor could I fee him after firing my carbine. Though I was fure I had hit him, it would have been been imprudent to have rufhed immediately into the thicket. As he made no noife, I fufpected he was dead or mortally wounded; " Friends," cried I to the hunters that approached, " let us go in a firm
" line ftrait up to him, if he is yet alive, all
" our pieces fired together will overcome
" him, and we can be in no danger;" one
" perfon only anfwered, and that was in the negative; in fhort, none liked the propofal. Enraged, I faid to my Hottentot (who was not lefs animated than his mafter) " com-
" rade, the animal is either dead, or near it,
" get on horfeback, approach as I did, and
" try to difcover in what ftate we have
" put him, I will guard the entrance, and
" if he attempts to efcape, will fhoot
" him,

"him; we shall be able to finish him without the assistance of these cowards." No sooner had he entered than he called to me that the tiger was extended, without motion, and he believed him dead; but to be assured, he fired his carbine; I ran, transported with pleasure: my brave Hottentot partook my exultation, triumph redoubled our force; we dragged the animal from the thicket, he seemed enormous; I examined him particularly, turning him from side to side, this was my first essay, and by chance, the tyger was monstrous; it was a male. From the extremity of the tail to the nose, he measured seven feet ten inches, to a circumference of two feet, ten inches. I found that he exactly answered the description of the Panther given by *Buffon*, but through all this country, he is known by no other name than the tyger, though it is only the prevalence of custom, for in this part of Africa, there are no tygers, the difference between that animal

animal and the Panther being very great. The Hottentots call it *garou gama*, or the *spotted lion*.

In general, in the colonies of the Cape, they fear the panther more than the lyon, the latter, never approaching without roaring terribly, himself giving a signal for preparation and defence; confiding in his strength, his attack is open; the others on the contrary, ever approach without noise, watch with art, and fall on their prey before it is aware of their appearance. I had many occasions afterwards of seeing different species of these animals; one called the *luypar*, by the Hollanders, which signifies leopard; another small one called the tyger cat, is the *ofclot* of *buffon*, of which I shall speak more hereafter.

When I had finished my remarks on the panther, and taken a drawing, we prepared

pared to skin him; my timerous companions drew near by little and little; it is true, they had reason to blush in the presence of a stranger, who on this occasion had shewn more intrepidity than any of those who were bred and born, if I may so speak, among the monsters of Africa. When we had finished our operation, my Hottentot wrapped the skin about him, and, saluting our hunters, we returned homewards, and walked in triumph, accompanied by several dogs whose masters had decamped at the beginning of the chace; they approached us fearfully, the tyger's skin keeping them in awe; sometimes the Hottentot turned, pretending to run at them, it was then a trial of skill who should run the fastest; this caused us a great deal of diversion.

Accounts of this expedition were soon spread, and I received some compliments
on

on my behaviour, even from thofe who had fo ill feconded me.

Soon after this expedition, another Colonift, who was unknown to me, and lived about four leagues off, fent to entreat that I would affift his fons in deftroying a panther that infefted his vicinity.

The experience I had gained on my firft effay, did not engage me to wifh for a fecond, I therefore declined the propofal, having refolved to expofe myfelf no more, to the danger of being the victim of another defertion; " No" anfwered I, " tell
" your mafter, I am not come into thefe
" countries to deftroy the race of tygers, I
" was too ill feconded in my firft attempt,
" for which reafon I fhall not wilfully en-
" gage in another; fhould chance lead me
" into a like fituation, I hope I fhall be able

"to defend myself without asking for af-
"siftance, therefore I shall not lend any."

But I was wrong for speaking thus haftily, and cenfuring thofe Colonifts I did not know, becaufe others had given me caufe of complaint; the invitation came from *Louis Karte*. Some time after I became acqainted with him, and was forry for the idea I had formed of his fons who proved themfelves as brave, as the others were daftardly, in the moment of danger.

The time I had purpofed being abfent from Mr. Boers, was almoft elapfed; the favorable feafon for my travels drew near; I had great preparations to make; I therefore took leave of the good *Slaber* and his family. I quitted them with regret, though free from care, embarrafsment, and inquietude, my heart lighter than when I came; I gave a laft look to the Bay of Saldanha, and took the road to the Cape.

CHAP.

CHAP. V.

THE CAPE MOUNTAINS, BAYS, AND COLONIES DESCRIBED—ACCOUNT OF THE NEGRO SLAVES—DIFFERENT SPECIES OF QUAILS &c.

MR. Boers expected me: on my arrival I became a part of his family. I found here every thing I could desire, without that haughty pride which so often impoisons the favors of the great. He even prevented my wishes by providing every necessary I stood in need of for my journey. I now began to prepare for it, and to that end cemented my friendship

with

he approved my expedition, he did not endeavour to hide from me the danger which attended the execution of it. The recital of the hazards encountered by himself on a like occasion only redoubled my ardor, and I belived myself invulnerable to those perils which he pourtrayed, and which were sufficiently discouraging. While my necessaries were preparing, I more particularly examined the town and its environs. I went several times upon Table and Lyon mountains; the former of them when viewed from the Bay, seems to join the town, though in fact it is at a league's distance from it. The foot of this mountain is incumbered with a great quantity of fragments of rock which seem at different times to have been broken from it; its base is formed of pure granite, and to its very summit, it is composed of horizontal layers of granite and earth alternately. Its height as computed by the *Abbe de La Caille*, is three thousand six hundred feet above the level of the sea;

and can only be climbed by the chasm, through which the water flows, which supplies the town; this passage is extremely dangerous, particularly towards the top, where it runs very narrow, and is almost perpendicular. It requires two good hour's labour to gain the summit, then you arrive at a very spacious plain confusedly scattered over with huge pieces of rock mingled with bushes, which altogether has the appearance of an immense city in ruins. Time in conjunction with the clouds and winds, has worn off their asperities, and given them a kind of uniformity. I have seen some stones there as compleatly rounded as those pebbles which are picked up on the sea shore. Towards the middle of the plain, there is a bason of three or four hundred paces in circumference, from whence the waters flow which supply the town by the channel before mentioned. I have taken a number of woodcocks here, whether this

water

water is supplied by springs, by rain, or by mists, is a question I cannot answer. The mountain is intersected by a number of channels which distribute the waters in every direction, and fertilize the scattered plantations which surround it. This place is the haunt of a great number of vultures, of that kind called perenoptere, they are frequently driven from the mountains by the South East wind with great precipitation into the very streets of the town where they are knocked down with sticks by the inhabitants. They also find here that kind of ape, which the Dutch call *bawians,* who are known to be very great thieves; and frequently get over garden walls, robbing them of the fruit, but never make their attacks with that order and precision that *Caille* speaks of in his childish and erroneous account of them. When the air is pure and serene one may distinguish from the top of Table mount, the mountains of *Piquet,* thirty leagues

leagues off; and though at so great a distance, they seem to surpass it in height. When people ascend Table mountain for the first time, while climbing the above mentioned chasm, they are sure to imagine that it rains, however fine the weather may be. This effect is caused by the water that is continually dropping from the rocks above, which in falling so far forms a kind of rain, which is ever more abundant in the morning, than the rest of the day; the damps and dews of the night easily account for this.

At about a third of the way up this chasm, the eye is presented with a beautiful cascade which falls from a flat piece of rock of considerable extent. From the town to this spot is a usual walk, even the ladies can proceed thus far without difficulty, and enjoy the satisfaction of a most charming and picturesque prospect which presents itself from this place.

The

The slaves frequently make a fire near where they are working, which serves them to light their pipes, and drefs their victuals. Thofe at the Cape, who are employed in cutting wood for their mafters firing (and who fometimes go for that purpofe to the other fide of Table mountain) when they leave work at night, often neglect to extinguifh the fires, which fpreading by means of dried roots and grafs, at length gain the woods, which taking fire, burn with violence, and difcharge clouds of flame and fmoke. The night following the town and road are prefented with a moft magnificent fpectacle, whofe caufe being known, the mind is not ftruck with that terror which fuch a phenomenon would otherwife occafion, for the elevation and extent of the fire, renders the mountain a much more tremendous fpectacle than Mount Vefuvius at the height of its eruption. I was never but once a witnefs of this majeftic illumination which I must confess threw me into an extacy. Whatever art has effected for the direction of vessels thirty leagues distance at sea, forms but a faint resemblance of this natural pharos lighted up by the carelessness of a poor negro. It is impossible to pass from Table to Devil mountain, though their summits seem only to have been separated by earthquakes, or some other cause; but you may easily go from that to Lyon mountain, which appears also to have been originally a part of the same, the top of the latter can only be gained by means of rope, with which, by great difficulty, they help themselves up; it is from this place that they give signals to ships at sea.

A servant of the company is always stationed here, who fires a cannon for every ship he discovers, and by a signal agreed on, they know in an instant whether the

vessel

vessel is coming from Europe or India. The same man as soon as he perceives what country it belongs to is obliged to go to town and inform the governor.

This employment is extremely dangerous, and it often happens that the poor fellow has to ascend and descend four or five times in a day, which is inconceivably fatiguing. This is a great cruelty in the government, which yet no one seems to think any thing of. The man I saw, told me with great tranquility, that they never grew old in this employment; I readily believed him, for though he was but thirty-five, his knees and ancles were so stiff, that he had enough to do to walk. I went likewise to visit the famous territory of *Constantia*, situate behind Table mountain. This vineyard does not however produce a tenth part of the wine that bears its name. It then belonged to a Mr. *Clocte*. Some say the original plants were brought from *Burgundy*, others that they came from *Maderia*, and others even from *Perfia*; thus much is certain, this wine is delicious at the Cape, but loses much of its goodnefs on being tranfported, and after five years old is good for nothing. At my arrival, the *Demi-Haam* (about eighty bottles) was fold from thirty-five, to forty piaftres; but at my departure the fame quantity was worth more than a hundred.

Not far from *Conftantia* there is another vineyard called *Litile Conftantia*, but it is only within feven or eight years, that the produce of this latter has equalled its neighbour, but lately it has arrived to fuch perfection, that it has even fetched the beft price at the Company's fales. As thefe plantations are only feparated by a hedge, the difference that arifes between their productions can only be the confequence of various modes of management.

The

The whole space between Table and False Bays, is interspersed with Summer houses, and beautiful habitations, where they cultivate vegetables, fruits and vines. The most esteemed, and whose produce approaches the nearest to the wine of Constantia are those of *Becker* and *Hendrik*. The Cape wine merchants purchase, and sell them for real Constantia. Besides their sweet wines, other cantons of the Colonies, as *Perle, Stellembosch*, and *Drageftein*, furnish those dry wines, which are in so great estimation. They make a wine here likewise which is very like *Rota*, and which is frequently called by that name, and I have drank some which has equalled the real. Those who wish to purchase at the Cape, must apply to those who cultivate it, if they would have good wine. For the merchants adulterate considerably, being sensible it will not keep in the casks, if they have not a ready sale, and in order to preserve it as long as as possible, they mix it with considerable quantities of brandy. The common wine of this country seldom makes its appearance at polite tables, red burgundy is most made use of, and the wine imported in Dutch vessels is always preferred to that brought by the French, which usually tastes of the cask, and will not keep. The average price of this wine is a florin a bottle, but it varies according to circumstances, and I have sometimes seen it sold for three florins, and at other times for twelve sous.

The beer they brew at the Cape is much esteemed, but they place a very high value on that which is brought from Europe, its price fluctuates from twelve to twenty-four sous the bottle; there is a great demand here for liquors in general.

On entering a house you are always presented with a *sopi*, that is to say, with a glass glafs of arrack, Geneva, or perhaps French brandy. Geneva, however, is the common morning dram. Before they fet down to table, the etiquette is to offer a *fopi* of white wine in which wormwood or aloes have been fteeped to create an appetite. At table they drink beer, or wine indifcriminately. After the defert the ladies retire to a different apartment, they then bring in pipes and tobacco, with a recruit of wine for the men; mean time the ladies are ferved with coffee, rhenifh, and mofelle. They then form themfelves into card parties, while the men continue to drink and fmoke, and if any interefting, or witty fubject is fta--ed among them, it is fure to furnifh a pretext for a few more bumpers. This is their ufual manner of living, with this difference, that thofe in indifferent circumftances drink their own wine, but in this particular, the vanity of the inhabitants is often very ridiculous; one day as I was walking with Mr. Boers, he made

made me obser[ve] a man seated at the door of his house, who seeing we were near him, began calling to his slave with a loud voice, to bring him some red wine, though the fiscal assured me, he had not a single bottle at his command, and that most likely he had not drank of it ten times in his life; when I had passed him some little way I turned and saw that it was beer his slave had brought him.

The Hout-Bay (or Wood Bay) takes its name from the wood that grows on its borders, which consists of bushy thickets, there being no large trees. This Bay is small, open to the West wind, and surrounded with rocks, it is rare for any vessels to anchor here, unless suddenly drove by bad weather, and unable to gain any other shelter; it is two leagues South-West of the Cape. False Bay, South-East of the Cape, is at the distance of three leagues, but it necessary to go four to

gain

gain good anchorage; this fpacious Bay is an afylum to a number of veffels; it is here the fhips from Table Bay take refuge when the Weft winds begin to blow, on the contrary, when the South Eaft commences they return to their former fituation.

The commander's appointment at Falfe Bay is but fmall, but his place is very profitable by the commerce he has with foreign veffels, buying their merchandife, which he fends to Cape town, where it fometimes fells for treble its value. On the borders of the Bay there are a number of large magazines in which are depofited provifion for the Company's veffels. likewife an hofpital for the crews, and an hotel for the governor, who ufually refides fome days there, when the fhips of the Company are at anchor. Commerce likewife draws a number from the Cape who furnifh lodgings for the officers; while the

the latter reside there, the Bay is very lively, but no sooner do they weigh anchor, than the place is deserted by all but the garrison which is relieved monthly. Ships who arrive after the other vessels departure are oftentimes rather unfortunate, the magazines being so compleatly emptied, that they who arrive last are obliged to produce what they want from the town, the carriage of which is exorbitantly dear, a miserable cart being from 20 to 30 piastres a day; I have seen even 50 given, but it is to be remarked that in twenty-four hours, they can make but one journey.

It is here they catch the best fish, particularly the *Kooman*, which gives its name to the rock near which it is found in great abundance; they likewise find oysters, but in small quantities. It must be remarked that on the land comprised between Table bay and Cape town, but above all near Constantia and New Land, is found the charming

charming tree called by the Dutch *silver blaaderen* (the protea argentea of the botanists:) it seems at the time Dr. Sparman resided at the Cape this tree was not in such quantities as at present, for the Colonists having remarked that it grew very fast, made large plantations of it; which are now become very useful to them for fuel. I observed that this tree grew in no other part of the colony, not even in the country of the Namaquois, from whence Mr. Sparman has supposed it first taken; I am assured it does not grow there, nor in any other of the Cantons that I have seen; I imagine it has been brought from some other part of Africa. Mr. Sonnerat in his last voyage to India, affirms it to be the only native of the Cape; it would seem that this naturalist had never seen the *mimosa nilotica*, which is very common there, as are a great number of others.

The colonies of *Stellenbosch, Drogestein, Fransche-Hoeek, La Perle, La Holland Hottentotte,*

tentotte, are different cantons situated between the Cape, and a great chain of mountains, these furnish all the fruit and wine. The Stellembosch is a little town where several inhabitants have retired from the Cape, who cultivate their own lands; they have a church, a minister, and a bailiff, who is a kind of judge to whom in case of debt or dispute they apply, but his power not enabling him to give greater damages than fifty rix-dollars, all above that sum must come under the cognizance of the fiscal. The Fransche-Hoeck in the heart of the mountains, between the *Stellembosch* and the *Drageftein*, has received its name from some refugees that settled there about the end of the last century. The land is good, and furnishes plenty of corn and wine. They make the best bread of all the colonies, not that the corn is better, but the French method of making it, which was introduced by the emigrants, and preserved from father to son, this appears the only remembrance left them of

their

their ancient and cruel country. I found, in this canton, but one old man who spoke French, yet several of the families bear and write their original names; there was among them that of *Malherbe, Dutoit, Retif, Cocher,* and many others that are familiar to us. They are only distinguished from the other Colonists (who are very fair) by their dark hair and brown complexions.

The division called *Dutch Hottentotte,* is so named because this Canton (originally inhabited by Hottentots) was the first that the Dutch seized on. It furnishes them with vegetables, fruit, and corn; the Stellembosch bounds it on the North, a chain of mountains on the East, False Bay, on the West, and the mountains where the natives still retain some habitations on the South.

The first chain of mountains that are seen from Table Bay are called the *Tiger Mountains,* on them are scattered excellent plantations for the growth of corn, which covering the hills, is a beautiful view from the town in the harvest season; their fruitfulness having given them the name of Corn Magazines to the whole colony.

The other side of these mountains are equally well cultivated; the farms in the neighbourhood of the Cape are generally very profitable, on account of the ease with which they convey their vegetables, fruit, eggs, milk, and all other necessary provisions to the town, an advantage which those at a greater distance do not enjoy.

For twelve leagues round the Cape the colonists do not employ Hottentots, rather buying Negroes who are not so lazy, and whom they can more safely trust. The Hottentots, careless and inconstant by nature, often go away on the approach of hard labour, and leave their masters in embarrasment; the Negroes desert also, but

but vain is their efforts for liberty, they are soon retaken, and sent to the Bailiff of the Canton, from whom the prosecutor reclaims them for a small fine, after they have received some trifling correction; nor is there any part of the world where the slaves are treated with such humanity as at the Cape.

The Negroes of Mosambique and Madagascar are regarded as the best workmen, and most affectionate to their masters; when they are landed at the Cape, they usually sell from a hundred and twenty, to a hundred and fifty piasters a head.

The Indians are more employed in houshold work in the town; there are also Malayans, who are the most subtle and dangerous of slaves. Assassinating their master or mistress is with them a common crime; during the five years I passed in Africa, I saw many instances of it. They go to execution with the greatest indifference. I heard one of these wretches say

say to Mr. Boers, he was glad he had committed the crime, that he well knew the death attending the commission of it, which he ardently wished for, as it would return him to his native country. I am amazed such an error does not cause greater misfortunes.

The Creole slaves at the Cape are most esteemed, they are sold at double the price of the others; and if they know any business, their price is exorbitant. A cook will sell from eight to twelve hundred rixdollars, and others in proportion to their talents. They are ever neatly dressed, but walk barefoot, as a mark of slavery. At the Cape there is none of that insolent train called footmen, luxury and pride not having yet introduced this useless lumber of the anti-chambers of the great.

A stranger is surprized on his arrival at the Cape, to see a multitude of slaves as fair as Europeans, but astonishment ceases when it is known the young female negroes

groes have generally a lover among the soldiers of the garrison, with whom they generally pass the Sunday; the interest of the master makes him overlook the morals of his slaves, he profiting by their licentious conduct.

There are, notwithstanding, female blacks, who are legally married, and negroes who form a part of the common people; they are men, who by their services, or from other motives, are emancipated; the facility with which they formerly gained their liberty, was subject to much abuse, as those who were old and infirm, on obtaining it, having no resource, became thieves and vagabonds; the government was obliged to take cognizance of this, and at present no master can free his slave without depositing a sum in the orphan charity for his maintenance.

One circumstance that causes depravity among the slaves, and will ever vitiate

tiate their morals, is, that the government of Batavia frequently send their disorderly slaves to the Cape. These people are generally Malayans, all thieves, or receivers, for the last article their reputation is so established, that their habitations are first searched when a slave is missing, or any property lost.

It is very uncommon for a master to punish a slave himself, he generally puts him into the hands of the fiscal, who orders him the necessary correction. If a master corrects his slave unmercifully, the latter may complain to the fiscal, who will oblige the master to sell him ; or in case of wounds or death, he is in danger of corporal punishment, or banishment to the Isle of *Roben*; these wise laws do honor to the Dutch government, but how many ways are there to elude them! Isle *Roben* is two leagues in the sea, in front of Table Bay, and in view of the town; it takes its name from the quantity of marine dogs that are found there.

This

This Isle is a flat of small extent, and is the place of banishment from the Cape; it is under the command of a corporal, who has the title of commander. The unhappy exiles are each day to deliver a certain quantity of lime-stone which they dig; in spare time they fish or cultivate their small gardens, which procures them tobacco and some other little indulgencies. It is astonishing to see how large all kinds of vegetables grow; cauliflowers are of an amazing bigness, and cultivated in sand; their goodness exceeds their size. There are likewise some violet coloured figs of exquisite smell. The wells furnish water as good as that at the Cape, an extraordinary phenomenon in an island of such small extent, and almost level with the sea.

I saw a great number of black serpents of four or five feet long, but they are not dangerous. Partridges and quails are found here in abundance, I have

some-

sometimes shot from fifty to sixty of a morning.

I must here make an observation interesting to Natural History; the quails of the Isle of *Roben*, and those of the Cape, are one and the same species, without the least difference that can render my assertion doubtful; notwithstanding the quail is a bird of passage, (a fact well known to every one) yet, though it is but two leagues from Isle *Roben* to Terra Firma, it is positively known that those birds never emigrate, being equally plentiful in all seasons. I must add, that the quails of Europe are absolutely of the same kind; then must we not conclude that the European quail never passes the sea, which has ever been asserted; some voyagers assure us they have seen them at sea, but that does not decide the question, for at seventy leagues from shore, I have shot from the yard of our vessel, starlings, chaffinches, linnets, and once an owl, all which birds are well known not to emigrate; they had doubtless been put to confusion by some hurricane or tempestuous weather; and I shall ever think the same of the quails, until that part of the history of birds has received more positive explanation. What makes me give less belief to their crossing the sea is, they may go to Africa by land, and return to Europe the same way; and surely if those of *Roben* Island dare not cross the little space that separates them from the Cape, much less would they risk a flight so very considerable. The quail is a very heavy bird, and the smallness of the wings proportioned to the weight of its body, badly calculated for a continued or long flight; and 'tis well known to every sportsman, that when a dog has raised a quail three or four times, it can no longer fly, but overcome with weariness, may be easily taken with the hand.

Besides the quail common in Europe and Africa, there is at the Cape a smaller bird, known also by the name of quail,
but

but very improperly; it has only three claws on each foot, and thofe placed before, which makes a fufficient difference to diftinguifh them.

Mr. Sonnerat, in his voyage to India, defcribes a bird of the fame fpecies, which he calls (caille a trois doigts). Mr. Deffontaines has likewife defcribed one on the coaft of Barbary, nearly refembling thofe of the Cape, of which no doubt there are great variety. I have feen two other kinds much larger, the one of Ceylon, the other of Java. I think they fhould be thrown into a feparate clafs, and ranged between the common quail and the duck, whofe feet have a fimilar formation.

The government fends every year a detachment into the Ifle of *Roben* to fhoot mors and manchets, which are called at the Cape, penguins, from whom they extract great quantities of oil. There is at
Ifle

Isle *Roten*, a little creek, which may afford shelter for one vessel when the South East wind hinders it from gaining the road of the Cape.

In quitting Europe I had no design to enter into minute descriptions of the manners and customs of the inhabitants of the Cape, much less of their form of government, political, civil, or military; this I confess did not form the principal part of my study, and it was with regret that I ran into such descriptions when they fell naturally in my way. I have as good reasons perhaps for my reserve in this point, as the reader can have for his curiosity. But even from the reveries of *Kolben* a number of useful remarks may be extracted. Ten years residence at the town could not fail of giving him sufficient opportunities of remarking their customs, and perhaps he has not imposed on his readers so much as some have imagined; customs which existed at the

the time he wrote, may have ceased, and his account of them be now considered as so many fables.

Manners, customs, laws, nay empires themselves are continually varying, so the account of any people, after a few ages, must be in the same predicament with a portrait, which though it may have been strikingly like a person in his youth, can hardly be said to retain any resemblance when the original is worn out with age.

What this traveller has advanced concerning the religious ceremonies of the Hottentots, has not the same plea, for I never could perceive that they had the least idea of a Being rendering retribution for vice or virtue. I have lived a long time with these peaceable people, I have penetrated a considerable way into their country, never did I see any trace of what has been affirmed concerning the customs they are said to observe on the birth of their male children, at their funerals, in their

their mode of legiflation, and above all, nothing of what they have been pleafed to affert refpecting their ridiculous and difgufting marriages.

Kolben is not yet forgot at the Cape; tis known that he never left the town, though he has fpoke with the certainty of an eye witnefs of the manners and cuftoms of the internal parts of the country.

It is however, not to be queftioned, but that after ten years refidence, and having done nothing of what he was charged with the care of, he thought it eafier to affociate with the good fellows of the colony, who, while they drank his wine, laughed in their fleeves, and vied with each other in recounting thofe ridiculous anecdotes which compofe the bulk of his memoirs. "Tis thus thofe new difcoveries were obtained which were to enlarge the bounds of human knowledge!

CHAP. VI.

DESCRIPTION OF THE AUTHOR'S TRAVELLING EQUIPAGE.—BEGINS HIS JOURNEY FROM THE CAPE.—VISITS THE HOT BATHS.—ARRIVES AT A HOTTENTOT HOORD.—ENCREASES HIS TRAIN.—JOURNEY CONTINUED.

I HAD got every thing in readiness for the journey; my baggage was confiderable; for in the firft ardor which had tranfported my imagination beyond its ordinary courfe, I had fet no bounds to my travels, but refolved to profecute them to the utmoft poffible extent, and wifhed above all things not to be conftrained to return for want of indifpenfible neceffaries. I knew too that my return might not be equally in my power with the departure; I had therefore taken care not to neglect even thofe things which were not abfolutely neceffary, but which might be ferviceable in a number of unforefeen circumftances, and I was even afraid of

for-

forgetting fomething, the want of which I might have occafion to regret.

The three months I had paffed at the Cape, fince my expedition to the Bay of *Saldanha,* had been fully employed in thefe neceffary preparations.

I had provided myfelf with two large four wheeled waggons, covered with a tilt. Five large chefts juft covered the bottom of one of the carriages, and I could readily open any one of them without difplacing the reft. On thefe was a mattrafs, which I propofed making ufe of as a bed during my journey, whenever it happened that want of time, or any other caufe prevented me pitching my tent. At the head of my mattrafs I placed a little cheft of drawers, which I meant fhould contain my infects, butterflies, or any other objects whofe tender texture might require care. I had fo well contrived thefe drawers, and my collection was

fo

so well preserved in them, that for the convenience of other naturalists, who may travel in similar circumstances, I have thought fit to describe the form. It was two feet and a half long, eighteen inches deep, and as many wide; the whole length was divided into eighteen departments, each of which contained a drawer that reached within three inches of the bottom; these drawers stood in a vertical direction, and were to be drawn out from the top, exactly filling the space designed for each, so that if the jolting of the waggon detached any of the insects from the frames to which I had fastened them, they could only fall into the before-mentioned space of four inches, and not incommode those that remained. Over the bottom of the box I spread a thin coat of virgin wax, tempered with linseed oil, which closed up the pores, and by its smell kept off the insects that might have injured my collection.

It was also in this first waggon that I stowed all my arms and ammunition, and we called it the *master waggon*; one of my before mentioned chests was divided into squares, each filled with a case bottle, containing five or six pounds of powder, besides which I had several barrels, which to preserve from fire, or moisture, I had caused to be sewn up in fresh sheep skins, which drying over the barrels, formed an impenetrable covering. I reckoned altogether that I had about five hundred weight of powder, and not less than two thousand weight of lead and pewter, wrought and unwrought; sixteen muskets, one of which I designed for the larger kind of animals (such as the Elephant, Rhinoceros and Hyppopotamus) was of a larger bore than ordinary, and carried a quarter of a pound of powder. I had besides these several pair of double barrelled pistols, a large cimiter and a dagger.

My second waggon contained a whimsical medley, but which was not on that account the less estimable. This was my kitchen. How many exquisite and peaceable repasts has it furnished me with! How pleasing are the details of this charming and domestic life to my heart! I never assist at those dinners where etiquette and tediousness preside, but the disgust they occasion brings to my remembrance my charming African meals, where my honest hottentots provided the banquet for their friend.

My kitchen furniture was not very considerable, a gridiron, frying pan, two saucepans and a large pot, some plates and dishes, coffee and tea cups, basons, two tea kettles, and a few other necessaries composed my whole equipage.

I had provided myself with a good stock of linen, plenty of sugar candy, and white sugar, coffee, tea and some pounds of chocolate.

As I was to furnish tobacco and brandy for the Hottentots that accompanied me, I had a large quantity of the first, and two casks of the latter; packages of glass and hardware to change occasionally, or procure the friendship of the natives; a large tent, and the necessary implements for mending my waggons, and for running of lead; an engine for raising weights, some nails, iron in bars, &c. with pins, needles, and thread, composed the second part of my travelling equipage.

My two waggons might weigh about five thousand pounds weight, and the astonishment they occasioned among the savages afforded me much amusement.

My train consisted of thirty oxen, twenty for the two waggons, and ten to relieve them occasionally; three horses for hunting, nine dogs, and five hottentots; my number of men and animals was occasionally

ally much increased, of the first sometimes to the number of forty. They were generally augmented or decreased, according to the state of my kitchen, for in the deserts of Africa, as in other and more polished countries, there are a number of Parasites; but these, without being much expence were not totally useless, as they furnished me with frequent opportunities of forming a judgment of the temper and genius of this people.

As my intended journey was known to all Cape Town; before my departure I was warmly solicited by several to permit them to accompany me, but these gentlemen and I thought very differently.

They imagined their proposal must give me a great deal of pleasure, they could not believe I would go only accompanied by Hottentots; on the contrary, I thought it not prudent to have any other companion, as I was not ignorant that of all the expeditions ordered by government, none had fucceeded; as a diverfity of tempers and characters can never fufficiently coincide; harmony in a new and hazardous expedition can hardly be maintained, among men, whofe felf love is ever predominant. I therefore was careful not to lofe the fruits of my voyage, and determined to go alone. I wifhed to be abfolute mafter in this expedition, which made me reject all their offers and keep firm to my purpofe.

My baggage being ready, I took leave of my friends, fetting out the 18th of December, 1781, on horfeback, at the head of my cavalcade; it was not my defign to make long ftages; I led the way towards *Dutch Hottentote*, and ftopped at the decline of day, at the foot of thofe high mountains that border the eaft of the cape.

It was neceffary to eftablifh regularity among my people, all depended on the beginning; without being a great philofopher, I knew enough of human nature to be aware of one truth, that whoever wifhes to be obeyed, fhould endeavour to render himfelf refpected, and in order to fucceed, fhould unite fortitude with vigilance. I had to guard againft being abandoned by my people, or fuffering them (by my weaknefs) to become diforderly; I therefore made ufe of a prudent referve, to which I ftrictly adhered, never relaxing, during my whole journey, from this neceffary precaution.

As foon as we ftopped I gave directions to put the things in order in my prefence, and under the infpection of two of my people on whom I had the moft reliance for exactitude. I now fent my beafts to graze, and took a review of my waggons and effects, to be affured all was in proper condition;

condition; I examined even the traces and harnefs, affigned each man his employ, holding at the fame time a fhort difcourfe on the different occupations they would hereafter have. From this they formed an idea of my carefulnefs and precaution, and felt that the leaft lapfe of duty would not efcape me; after this ceremony I mounted my horfe, and went to reconnoitre the road over the mountain, which we were to pafs on the morrow. On my return I found the oxen difpofed of as I had ordered, and a good fire burning; we fupped lightly on fome provifions we had brought from the town, I in my waggon, the hottentots in the open air.

We were ready by day break to begin our journey over the mountains, at the rifk of breaking our waggons, and laming our beafts; at length we gained the fummit. The road is full of chafms, fteep, and fo befet with broken pieces of rock, that

that I could not but wonder how the only road by which the inhabitants of thefe cantons ever arrive at the Cape fhould be fo neglected. There is a furprifing profpect from the top of this mountain, comprifing all the plantations which are fcattered over an extenfive hollow, formed between this and the oppofite chain of mountains, quite to the fea.

We were obliged to unyoke the oxen, to give them fome hours reft, and wifhing to gain the plain by fome eafier defcent, I profited by this fhort interval, and reconnoitred the fpot. I was perfectly fatisfied when I perceived the defcent on the other fide to be an eafy pleafant flope, which would lead us, without danger, into a delightful country; the road was really commodious and eafy for our waggons, and we defcended with as much eafe and pleafure as we had pain and difficulty in our afcent. The wild beafts feldom fhew
themfelves

themselves in these cantons, having therefore nothing to fear, we travelled until ten o'clock at night, when we arrived on the borders of the river *Palmit*, thus named by the Dutch, on account of the many reeds that grow on the borders.

In the morning, on our waking, we sought in vain for the oxen; they had disappeared, being not yet accustomed to rest by the side of our carriages. My people went in quest of them, and it took so much time to re-assemble them, that we were not ready for our departure until nine o'clock in the morning; about eleven we passed within fifteen paces of a habitation; the master of it no sooner saw my caravan than he came out to meet me. I found it to be the person from whom I had bought, at the Cape, my master waggon, and the five pair of oxen that drew it. I was obliged to stop and accept the pressing invitation he gave me to dine; especially when

when he informed me, that having learned at the Cape, on the day of my departure, what road I meant to take, he had set out immediately to prepare for my reception. I ordered my oxen to be unyoked, and went home with him, where I was received by his wife and daughters with great civility.

Viewing this plantation, and listening to his praises on the waggon he had sold me, with a recapitulation of the good qualities of the oxen that drew it, employed me till dinner time. To his honor he did not exaggerate; for I have since found those beasts much better than any others I have employed, and his waggon, being constructed with skill, ever resisted the roughest shocks in my hazardous journey.

Notwithstanding the entreaty of this good family to pass the night with them, I de-

I departed when I had dined. A few hours after we croffed the river *Bott*, and paffed the whole of the canton called *Ouwe Hoeck*. I wifhed to regain the time loft at dinner, and it was eleven o'clock at night before we ftopped at the fide of a fmall ftanding water.

The fun was hardly rifen when we recommenced our journey, and halted in the morning near the habitation of *Francis Bathenos*; he fent me a loaf that I wanted, but it was in vain to offer any thing for it: He likewife entreated me to come to his houfe; but I defired to be excufed, not caring to pafs my time in thefe habitations. I faw in this country a prodigious number of Gazells, which the colonifts call *Reebock*, which is yet but little known. Mr. Sparman has only mentioned them. The name of this animal, in the French tranflation of that work, is, by miftake,
rendered

rendered *Red Bock*, which this word does not fignify.

The heat of the fun at mid-day was exceffive, and obliged us to halt; in the mean time I took a fhort turn, and was fortunate enough to kill a *Reebock*.—The general colour is a light grey, darker on the back than the fides, the belly white, its horns are only five or fix inches in length. Mr. Sparman, who fays he only wrote from memory, was miftaken in faying, they were a foot long. The defcription and figure of this animal is to be found in my *Treatife on the Quadrupedes of Africa*.

I returned to my people.—We ftayed no longer than was juft neceffay to broil fome part of my game. And in the fpace of four leagues, which we afterwards went to gain a commodious encampment, we had on all fides, very near us, Gazells, Bontibocks,

Bontiboeks, (the *Antelope Scripta* of Mr. Pallas) Bubales (the Antelope Bubalis) with numbers of Zebras, Oftrichs, &c. &c.

The variety and appearance of this large troop of animals was extremely amufing, and highly worthy the pen of a naturalift.

My dogs eagerly purfued thefe creatures, who mingled as they fled, and altogether formed one vaft herd; but the moment I had called off my dogs, and they thought themfelves out of danger, each different fpecie compofed a feparate band, and kept at a cetain diftance from each other.— Had it not been for my dogs, who always kept them at a diftance, I could have fhot numbers of them from my waggons, for they were very tame, and feemed pleafed to gaze on us.

Indeed,

Indeed, a kind of curiosity approaching to familiarity, seems to be the characteristic of all horned animals, particularly the Gazell. There were only the Zebras, and the Ostriches that kept at a greater distance. I was now within four or five leagues of the hot baths so much cried up and visited by the inhabitants of the Cape. I was anxious to see them; but I was afraid my journey would be too much retarded by it. To gain, therefore, on the one hand what I lost on the other, I resolved to set out earlier in the morning than usual; by ten o'clock we reached them.

This spring of mineral waters, so generally esteemed, is about thirty leagues distance from the Cape. Government has raised a very spacious and convenient building, for the use of those valetudinarians who frequent those baths. Lodging, it is true, costs nothing here; but the invalid is obliged to provide necessaries, and these are

are not very easily procured in this country.

There is in this place two baths, the one for the whites, the other for blacks, and the mountain called the *Tower* of *Babel*, is not far from this place, whose height *Kolben* has so greatly exaggerated; I suppose 'tis nearly as high as table mountain. All round this mountain the company have got enclosures, where, under the inspection of an officer appointed for that purpose, they fatten large herds of cattle, with which they victual their shipping.

I crossed, the next day, the river *Steenbock*, not far from which is a beautiful habitation of the widow *Wissel*; and just after I crossed a second river; in passing this I saw the hospital designed for the company's cattle.

They

They fometimes get cured here, but in other refpects this eftablifhment is of great utility, as it prevents contagious diforders from infefting thofe who are healthy, and from whom they are feparated immediately on their fhewing any figns of indifpofition.

I had refolved to travel the greater part of the night, but was obliged to ftop at nine o'clock, in the valley of *Soete-Melck*, which is a deep morafs; fearing to proceed, as it would have been highly imprudent to have attempted croffing it during the night. Early in the morning I faw a very pretty houfe at a fmall diftance from us; it was a poft belonging to the company, and commanded by M. *Martines*. I knew him by having feen him at the Fifcal's. I went to vifit him; like the reft of the colonifts, he would fein have engaged me to remain there fome days;

but

but my impatience to continue our route made me decline it.

About mid-day I paſſed a little *Horde* belonging to ſome Hottentots, who appeared ſo poor and miſerable, that it induced me to make them ſome little preſents.— They had not a ſingle beaſt, but lived by labouring in the neighbouring plantations. I invited ſome to accompany me, promiſing to pay them well on my return; but my perſuaſions were uſeleſs, until I had aſſured them they ſhould have a ſufficient quantity of tobacco the whole way; they then promiſed to be with me the next day.

I paſſed the night at *Tiger Hoek*, where I waited for my recruits 'till nine o'clock in the morning, I had juſt given them up, and was preparing to purſue my journey, when three of them arrived with their arms and baggage; this little reinforcement gave me great pleaſure, they mixed

with the others and were soon acquainted. I delayed my departure until the afternoon, as I wished to view the country; one of my new comers requested to accompany me, with assurances that he was an excellent huntsman. I had brought from Europe the common opinion formed of people who praise themselves, and did not set a very high estimate on my Hottentot's abilities; however I ordered him a gun, and we set out together. We soon met with a flock of Gazells, the face of the country was absolutely covered with them, but they kept out of gun-shot. After having run a long time to no purpose, my companion stopped suddenly, telling me he saw a *Blawe Bouc*, (a blue Bock.) Laying down I turned my eyes the way he directed, but could not see it; he desired me to stand quite still, assuring me he would soon give a good account of it; he then turned from me, creeping on his knees. I did not lose sight of him. His method of hunting

ing being quite new, engaged my attention. The animal at length arose, and began grazing; it had to me the appearance of a white horse, for at the distance I then was, it looked entirely of that colour. I had never before seen any of this kind of Gazells, however I was undeceived when I saw the horns; my hottentot approached so near that the surprise of the animal and the firing of his piece were instantaneous; the Gazell fell, and I ran with haste to contemplate at my ease the most scarce and beautiful species of the African Gazells. I assured my Hottentot I would recompense him on my return to the camp. I then sent him for a horse to carry home our game. The knowledge this man had shewn in surprising the animal, rendering his service important and necessary, determined me to engage him by all the little baits that delight the Hottentots; I gave him a good stock of tobacco, a steel, some tinder and one of my best knives,

knives, which he immediately began to ufe, fkining the animal with as much dexterity as he had fhot it.

CHAP. VII.

DESCRIPTION OF THE GAZELL—OF THE TORTOISE — MANNER OF TAKING THEM — THE AUTHOR'S MONKEY DESCRIBED.

THIS Gazell has been defcribed by *Pennant*, under the name of the blue Antelope; and by *Buffon*, under that of the Tzeran. This laft mentioned naturalift has added a drawing of part of its horns;

horns; it is scarce and very little known, for during the whole time of my being in Africa, I never saw but three, and one of these was presented to the Governor some years after while I resided at Cape Town; it came as well as mine from the valley *Soete-Melk*, the only canton where they are to be found. I had been assured there were some in the country of the great *Namaquois*; but notwithstanding all my information and enquiries, I found I had been deceived in this particular; for all the savages which inhabit that country have assured me they knew nothing of it. I had been informed likewise that the females had horns as well as the males. I can say nothing to this, as all I saw were of the latter sort. Their prevailing colour is light blue, rather inclining to the grey; the belly and the whole inner part of the legs are as white as snow, and its head is beautifully spotted with white. I never remarked that the skin of this animal while

while living, resembled blue velvet, but changed its colour when dead; as we are assured by M. Sparman. Dead or living I never perceived any difference; the colour of those I had never varied. I have seen one of them at Amsterdam, (which they have had there these fifteen years) that exactly resembles the Governor's, at the Cape; it is in better preservation than mine, but in other respects the same. I cannot help adding in this place, that I did not know this animal from the engravings I had formerly seen of it. With my description I shall give a very exact drawing of this creature, taken on the spot.

The next day, the air being fresh and pleasant, we travelled for six hours, till we gained the borders of a considerable lake, which abounds in little tortoises; we caught about twenty of them, and when broiled they are excellent food. They are about seven or eight inches long, and four inches over;

over; the shell is of a light grey colour, rather inclining to yellow; while living they have a difagreeable fmell which is loft in dreffing.

It is remarkable that when the exceffive heats have dried up all the water, in proportion as the furface becomes dry, the Tortoifes bury themfelves at different depths in the earth, where, if not difturbed, they remain in a torpid ftate, neither fhewing themfelves nor awaking 'till the return of the rainy feafon. They lay their eggs in the open air, on the borders of the fmall lakes and moors, and leave to the fun the care of hatching them. Thefe eggs (which are about the fize of thofe laid by pigeons) are very well tafted, the white never hardens from dreffing, but remains a tranfparent blue jelly.

I am unacquainted whether this method of burying themfelves is an inftinct common-mon to all the different fpecies of Tortoifes, but I found, whenever I had an inclination for any of thefe, that it was only neceffary to turn up the earth in the places where the water had remained longeft, when I never failed to procure as many of them as I pleafed.

This kind of Tortoife hunt, if I may fo call it, was not new to me; when at Surinam I remember to have feen the fame ftratagem made ufe of to take two fpecies of fifh, the one called *Varrappe*, the other *Gorret*, or *Kwikwi*, which likewife bury themfelves in the earth.

Our waggons, which were placed on the borders of the lake, affrighted the Gazells that frequented it, and prevented them from drinking. The Bontibocks, efpecially, come for this purpofe, to the number of two thoufands in a flock; and I am perfuaded, that of Bubales, Gazells of all fpecies, species, Zebras and Ostrichs, I had in my view, at one time, not less than four or five thousand. I only wished for an Ostrich, but it was impossible to approach them. The other animals, though fearful, were often within gun shot; but as I was not in want of provisions, I did not wish to destroy them.

There was only the *Breed-river* and the *Klip-river*, between Swillendam and the spot I now occupied; I wished to see that colony, where I intended to pass some days, and take a particular view of all the animals I had collected. I set off accordingly, and we arrived there early the next day.

Of all the rivers we had crossed in this country, the *Diep-river*, and the *Breed-river* are the most considerable; the others scarcely deserve the name of rivulets during the heats, though, in the rainy season, they

they swell to furious torrents, and cut off all communication with the Cape.

I stayed several days at Swellendam, with Mr. Ryneveld, bailiff of the place, who treated me with the greatest civility. I found my two waggons were overloaded, and wished to procure some other carriage; this generous host had one constructed with two wheels, which, at my departure, he presented me with, and likewise a profusion of fresh provision.

I hired some additional Hottentots; recruited my stock of live animals with several oxen, some goats, a cow to furnish me with milk, and a cock; this last I considered as a kind of natural alarm, which would serve to wake me of a morning.

Every naturalist, I might say every country clown, knows that the cock crows
regularly

regularly in the courſe of the night, at the ſame hour; and that he never fails to announce the approach of day.

I can't conceive that there was any thing to ridicule in this precaution, which, if not neceſſary, was, at leaſt amuſing; yet the critics, in more than one public paper, have been pleaſed to divert themſelves at my expence, on that account. They have aſſured the public in my name, that I meant the cock ſhould ſerve as a ſubſtitute for my watch, in caſe it happened to be deranged by any accident. They have added, with the ſame temper, in another place, that "meeting for the firſt time with a lion, we gazed proudly on each other, and then paſſed quietly on, mutually ſatisfied with our majeſtic countenances." But, notwithſtanding theſe gentlemen choſe to be pleaſant on the occaſion, I found my expectations, in behalf of the cock, were not deceived; he ever rooſted

roosted on my tent, or waggon, and regularly announced the first appearance of aurora; he soon became familiar, and never wandered from my camp; or if, in search of provision, he strayed farther than usual, the approach of night constantly brought him back. When pusued by a small quadruped, of the pole-cat kind, I have seen him, half running, half flying, make the best of his way home, and crying, as if for help, with all his might; when one or other of my dogs never failed to hasten to his rescue.

An animal which rendered me still more essential service, whose diverting presence has suspended, nay, even dissipated a number of disagreeable and painful reflections; and whose provident instinct seemed to outstrip the efforts of my reason, was a monkey, of that kind commonly known at the Cape under the name of *Bavians*. He was very familiar, and particularly attached

attached to me; I made him my taster. Whenever we found any fruits, or roots, unknown to my Hottentots, we never attempted to eat them 'till they had been prefented to *Kees*, and if rejected by him, we concluded they were either difagreeable, or dangerous, and abandoned them accordingly. Animals of the monkey kind feem diftinguifhed from others by their fimilarity to the human fpecies.

Nature has furnifhed this creature with an equal quantity of gluttony and curiofity; without appetite he will tafte every thing that is prefented to him; without neceffity he will examine every thing he can lay his paws on. *Kees* poffeffed another quality ftill more eftimable than thofe I have already mentioned: His extreme vigilance rendered him my greateft fafeguard both day and night. The approach of the fmalleft danger roufed him in an inftant; by his cries and frighted geftures

we

we received intimation of the enemy, even before my dogs suspected it. They were accustomed to his voice and manner, and seemed to rely so much on his care, that they slept at their ease; and I was not without my fears, that if death should deprive me of my faithful guardian, I should not find that security from them I had flattered myself with, and which I thought I had a right to expect. When once *Kees* had raised them, they seemed very attentive to his signals; they watched his eyes and motions, and I observed never failed to run all together towards the spot that his looks were directed to. I often took him a shooting with me; what gambols! what expressions of joy! would he manifest on seeing me prepare to depart: he would leap upon and caress me, seeming by his looks and actions to entreat me to hasten my departure, and express his gratitude for admitting him to be of my party.

During

During our journey he would amuse himself with climbing the trees to search for gum, which he was very fond of; sometimes he discovered honey in the crevices of the rock, or in hollow trees; but when he happened not to find any thing of this sort, and his appetite, sharpened by fatigue and exercise, urged him more forcibly to seek a supply, a scene commenced which, to me, was extremely entertaining: In these emergencies he would dig for roots, which, when found, were presently demolished. He seemed particularly fond of a kind which, unluckily for him, I also found extremely good and refreshing, and ever obstinately persisted in partaking with him.

Kees was artful; and if he happened to find any of this root when I was at a distance from him, in order to prevent my coming in for my share, would eat it up with the greatest.

greatest eagerness, fixing, at the same time, his eyes ardently on me; and seeming to calculate, by the distance I was at, the time I should be getting to him. I observed his haste was ever in proportion to the danger he supposed he run of losing a part of his prize; and, in general, he was too quick for me; but sometimes, having found more than he had time to make away with, he would endeavour to conceal it on my coming up with him; on these occasions I usually favoured him with a good box on the ear, which never failed to make him give up the residue, when he was obliged to content himself with the part I chose to allot him. *Kees* never entertained any animosity, though I sometimes gave him occasion, by keeping the whole, to reflect on that greedy selfishness of which he had set the example.

He had a very ingenious method of coming at these roots, which used to

amuse

amuse me extremely: He took the tuft of leaves between his teeth, then bearing upon his fore paws, forced back his head, and generally drew out the root to which they adhered. When this means, which required all his strength, happened to fail, he again took hold of it closer to the earth, and giving a sudden spring, never failed to draw it up with him.

In our walks, when he found himself fatigued, he would mount upon the back of one or other of my dogs, who usually had the complaisance to carry him, even for hours together; but there was one among them bigger and stronger than the rest, and who ought rather to have offered his service on these occasions, that had a droll method of getting rid of his burthen: The moment he felt *Kees* upon his shoulders he became immoveable, and suffered me to proceed with the rest of the dogs without stirring from the spot. *Kees*, rather obstinate

obstinate on his part, would usually maintain his feat 'till I had almost got out of sight; when, fearful of being left behind, he was constrained to alight; and then both monkey and dog used to set off full speed to rejoin us; but I observed the dog always let *Kees* keep a head, taking care that he should not surprise him a second time. He had acquired over the rest of my pack an ascendency, which was, doubtless, owing to the superiority of his instinct; for with animals as among men, it is frequently observable, that address subdues strength.

Kees never cared to have company at his meals; and when any of my dogs approached too near his mess, he was sure to treat them with a box on the ear, which was always sufficient to make the cowardly animals make the best use of their legs.

One

One fingularity which I never could account for, was, that next to the ferpent, he was moft afraid of his own fpecies. Whether he was fenfible that his prefent domeftic ftate had deprived him of part of his faculties, or was fearful that any other fhould partake of my kindnefs; for I could eafily have taken fome wild ones, and tamed them; but I never had any fuch intention; I had an attachment for *Kees*, which prevented my wifhing for any other of his kind.

He fometimes heard the monkeys fcreaming in the mountains; and, notwithftanding his fears, feemed inftinctively to anfwer their cries; but when any one appeared, he ran with the utmoft precipitation, and trembling with fear, feemed to implore our protection.

At thefe times we always had enough to do to calm his terror. He was a great thief,

thief, which is a fault common to domestic animals; but in *Kees* this vice seemed a talent, the ingenuity of which I could not help admiring. My people, who were not always inclined to take his thieveries in good part, frequently corrected him; but it was all in vain, they never could reform him in this particular. He knew perfectly well how to untie the cords which fastened the baskets, in order to help himself to provision, especially milk, which he was very fond of, and several times, in consequence of this, I have been obliged to go without. I sometimes beat him myself for his mischievous tricks, after which he usually made his escape, and would not return to the tent 'till it began to grow dark.

I have hung on these details with pleasure. If they do not tend to the instruction of mankind, they are interesting to a soul like mine, delighted with the most simple

simple objects; recollecting with pleasure my innocent pastimes, my days of peace, and only moments of my life in which I was sensible of the whole value of my existence.

CHAP. VIII.

FIDELITY OF A DOG—THE AUTHOR'S REFLECTIONS ON LIBERTY—MANNER OF PASSING HIS TIME IN CAMP—REMITS HIS COLLECTION TO THE CAPE—CROSSES A RIVER ON RAFTS—ARRIVES AT MUSCLE BAY.

WHILE I remained at Swillendam, the friendly behaviour of my host inspired me with the liveliest gratitude; but

but it was a life not suiting my humour, therefore, as soon as my cart was finished, I placed in it my kitchen utensils, and without delay proceeded on my journey, on the 12th of January, 1782. From the information I had gained, I took an easterly course, keeping a convenient distance from the sea. The corn farms reached no further on this side, the moderate price that article bears, not being equivalent to the expence and difficulty of sending it to town.

I passed a little river called *Buffias*; and after two days journey, arrived at a wood named *le Bois de grand Pere*. I determined to stay here 'till the next day, and prepared accordingly, wishing to explore the wood. In calling my dogs, I observed that a little bitch, named Rosette, which I was very fond of, was wanting. Concerned at its absence (as it was a real loss to my pack) I enquired of all my people

whether

whether they had seen her on the road; one, only, assured me he had fed her in the morning. After an hour or two spent in fruitless searches, I sent out my Hottentots to call on all sides, and fired my piece several times, thinking the report might reach, and put her on the scent. When I saw these endeavours did not succeed, I ordered one of the men to mount my horse, and return the way we came, directing him to spare no pains in tracing my favorite.

In about four hours we saw the messenger returning on the full gallop, carrying before him, on the pommel of the saddle, a chair and a large basket; Rosette was running before, appearing as pleased to see me, as I was satisfied with her return.

The Hottentot informed me he had found her at about two leagues distance, seated

seated in the road, by the side of the chair and basket, which had dropped from our waggon without being perceived. I had heard much of the fidelity of dogs, in similar cases; but this was the first instance I had ever witnessed.

I own the little recital affected me; and the proof she had given of her attachment made her still more valuable. If my man had not been successful in his search, she must have perished with hunger, or have been a prey to some wild beast. The guns I had fired to bring her in sprung no game; and a survey of the forest convinced me we should find none on this spot; I determined, therefore, to continue our route on the morrow.

We had travelled about four leagues, when in crossing a river, my cart overset, and the rest of the day was employed in diving after, and drying, my kitchen furniture, and

and the other utenfils it contained. A great part of my china, which was broken, we left behind; very fortunately, I had a referve in the waggon.

In the evening we purfued our way for three leagues: we were then ftopped by the river *Duyvengchs*, which was not fordable at that time. The country round being covered with wood, I flattered myfelf I fhould meet with fome curious birds and infects; therefore refolved to wait here 'till the river funk, and ordered my Hottentots to pitch the tents on the border of the wood, and erect fome huts for themfelves.

The inhabitants of the environs hearing of my arrival, came with great kindnefs on a vifit. Though it was difturbing me in this charming retreat, I was obliged to bear their obliging reproaches, for not vifiting their habitations, to which
they

they urged me by every possible method; telling me the number of curious travellers they had entertained; and naming, among others, Mr. Sparman. Though the example was very respectable, I could not be persuaded to leave my camp. I determined, in the future course of my travels, not to stop at any habitation; to be free day and night; to have, perpetually, under my inspection, my attendants and carriages; in short, not to sacrifice my time, which was precious, to the absurd recitals, foolish tales, and idle questions, with which the colonists abound. It was likewise necessary to be sparing of my brandy, with which I was ever obliged to wet their uninteresting, tedious discourses; I therefore thanked the gentlemen for their kind invitations; but at the same time strictly adhered to my resolution.

The example of Mr. Sparman was nothing to me; our pursuits were different, conse-

consequently our ideas were not likely to accord; the day was sufficient for his botanical searches, but I frequently passed whole nights in hunting, and should, therefore, have been obliged to disturb and otherwise derange my entertainers, or alter my custom, neither of which I should easily have submitted to. Another motive, purely personal, may, in a few words, give a true idea of a temper which instigated me to this plan of life; and if the reader finds a trait of self-love in it, my age, my country, education, and the difficulties I have encountered, must plead my excuse.

I acknowledge, the force of custom in civilized society, is often pleaded by those inanimate beings who chuse to saunter on in one dull uniform track; but habituated at Surinam from my youth to freedom, every infringement (to me) seemed a tax on liberty. Man, justly proud of his superiority over the irrational creation, should

not

not be circumscribed in his steps, and I have ever cautiously avoided beaten paths, or fixed maxims.

In the midst of the deserts, surrounded by the rocks and forests of Africa, my independence was compleat; there I was sure to see no trace of human art but what myself should form; it was there I truly found that man was lord of the creation. This humour marked the early part of my life, and is the pure and natural sentiment of liberty, which repulses with disdain every infringement on its right; many reasons attached me to these principles, and I so well adhered to them, that I never broke on my original plan but once, during my travels.

To give some idea of our order and usual occupations, when we put up at night, I slept in my tent, or waggon; at break of day, awakened by the crowing of my cock,

I prepared coffee for breakfast, while my Hottentots on their part were employed in cleaning and preparing the oxen; at sunrise I took my gun, and attended by my monkey, searched about until ten o'clock, on our return I ever found the tent clean swept; this was particularly the business of an old African, called Swanepoel, who was not able to follow us on foot, therefore stayed behind to keep all in order.

I had not much furniture in my tent, the utensils consisted of two chairs, a table, on which I dissected my animals, and some instruments for preparing them. I usually employed myself that way from ten 'till twelve o'clock, or in arranging the different insects I had procured in the drawers. My method of dining was not very sumptuous; I placed on my knee a bit of plank covered with a napkin, and was then served with a single plate of roast or boiled meat; this frugal meal ended, I returned to to my work, if I had not finished it before, after which I went a hunting 'till sun set. On my return I passed some hours in seting down in the journal, my observations, acquisitions, and all the transactions of the day; during this time my men were employed in gathering the cattle round the tent; my goats, after being milked, laying down to sleep with the dogs.

Our business done, and a great fire made, we sat down in a circle, and while I was taking tea, the men were smoaking their pipes, and telling stories so very ridiculous, that they occasioned me much mirth. I took great pleasure in seeing them chearful, and my freedom and good humour banished in those meetings timidity and fear; the dispute then was whose story should most amuse, and the profound silence which reigned among us, might have flattered the most expert reciter.

Sometimes

Sometimes indeed, more pleafed with my own reflections, I felt myfelf drawn by an involuntary impulfe to contemplate the beauties of a calm and ferene evening, after the heat and fatigues of the day. In what lively colours does memory frequently paint thofe charming peaceful habitations! Methinks I am feated in my camp, furrounded by my people, a plant—a flower—a piece of rock, fcattered here and there—nothing efcapes my recollection, and the charming idea interefts, amufes and delights me.

Sometimes our difcourfe led us beyond the ufual hour, and I muft own, thefe uneducated people had often ftrokes of wit and humour in their converfation that furprifed me: I queftioned them particularly on Colben, and the different accounts authors give of their religion, laws and cuftoms; fome of thefe interrogatories would occafion them to laugh in my face, at other times

times they were downright angry, supposing these enquiries were meant either to teaze, or undervalue their faculties and knowledge. I sometimes described that set of beings, who in great cities, procure by their finesse an elegant subsistence, and are entitled *Chevaliers d'Industre*; I represented in a thousand forms the tricks of these camelions, and painted them in the most flattering colours; with what pleasure did I see my Hottentots unanimously prefer the simplicity of their country to these seducing pictures; looking on such resources as vile and illiberal in men, who boast a superiority over those who are only instructed by nature.

Worthy injured people! whom so many have taken pleasure to represent as unnatural monsters, devouring each other, an infant might lead ye! Peaceful Hottentots! behold with disdain those harsh invaders who first reduced to slavery, then

basely

basely traduced and placed ye on a level with the brutes.

My animals were so accustomed to mix with us, that I was frequently obliged to disturb several before I could enter my tent. I had some sheep which I reserved in case of scarcity; and I took particular care of some old ones who were very serviceable in accustoming the new comers to feed near my camp.

This part of the country abounded with partridges, they were of three different species, one of which was as large as a pheasant; these were our common food, and we frequently boiled twenty at a time, which mode of cooking afforded excellent broth.

Here was also a species of Gazells, about the size of our European goats, whose skins were of a dark brown, with some spots

spots of white on the thighs; they were very fine food. I also shot several of another kind, much smaller, and which I shall hereafter describe.

My stay in this place had considerably augmented my collection of insects, and curious birds; a colonist in the environs who was going to the Cape, offered his service if I had any commands; I accepted it with great satisfaction, consigning to his care my little treasure, to be taken to M. Boers. I had told that gentleman, if opportunity offered, I would remit my collection in parcels as I could to him, since by that means they would be in safety, and make room for others I might gather.

My neighbours used often to send me presents of vegetables, or fruits, and Mr. Vanwerck, who lived near my camp, knowing I was fond of milk, sent me a pailful every night, which I shared with my people.

Kees

Kees ever scented the carrier at a distance, and hastened to meet him.

From *Swellendam* to *Duyvenochs*, the pastures are good, and the land much superior to that near the Cape; it produces excellent corn, and in great quantities, but the colonists cultivate no more than serves for their own consumption, supplying the Cape only with beasts and butter. There are likewise some vinyards, but the wine is bad, serving only for the Brandy or Vinegar which is consumed in the neighbourhood.

On the twenty-seventh, the river being greatly sunk, we crossed it without danger, and also False River. After thirteen hours travel we reached that of the *Geus*, or *Gourits*, where we were obliged to stop, for it was impossible to cross it, being as wide as that part of the Seine that fronts the King's-gardens, at Paris. Some great inundation

inundation must have overwhelmed part of the country, through which it takes its course; for in this season it is ordinarily like the others, a fordable rivulet. On the borders grow quantities of large thorny trees, as the *Mimosa, Nilotica*; it likewise abounds with partridges, of that kind which the inhabitants of the Cape call *Fesants*.

After three days encampment, as the river did not sink, and being impatient to continue my rout, I determined to construct a raft, and for that purpose felled some large trees; the bark answering the purpose of cordage. This was a work of infinite labour, being obliged to unload, take our waggons to pieces, and carry them and the goods over at several turns; the cattle swam the stream in perfect safety, neither they, the people, or effects sustaining the least injury.

This attempt anfwering fo well, gave me freſh courage, though it coſt us three days hard toil, not allowing us even time for hunting: In all our labour I ever fet the example, working as much as any of the Hottentots; in this inſtance it was particularly neceſſary, for our common fafety, to uſe difpatch in quitting our fituation, which was fo barren, that had our ſtay been prolonged, the cattle muſt have periſhed with hunger.

The waggons being put together and reloaded, we continued our way, travelling fourteen leagues in two days, which brought us to Muſcle Bay, this in the charts bears the name of *Bay Saint Blaiſe*; the anchorage here is very difficult, on account of the craggy rocks that furround it, and extend far into the fea; but on the Northfide there is a flat ſhore, of no great extent, where ſhallops may approach with fafety.

A number of good habitations are scattered about the adjoining country, which are a resource to vessels that anchor in the bay. We here procured Oysters in great quantities; sometimes we angled, and by this means furnished ourselves with plenty of excellent fish, as we had more than we could use, I caused part of them to be salted.

Every night we heard the howlings of the Hyæna, which terrified our oxen, but by means of the great fires that surrounded our camp, we kept them at a distance.

A league from this place there is a *Kraal*, of about four huts, belonging to a Hottentot family, consisting of twenty-five people; I changed some tobacco with them for mats, which I much wanted. I was pleased with my discovery of this little settlement, not for the necessaries I received of them, but for the advantage of

considering

considering their peaceful manners. They had five cows and a small flock of sheep; in the proper season the men laboured in the neighbouring plantation, earning what procured them tobacco, and other little necessaries.

They assured me, that in the woods (with which the mountains are covered) they sometimes meet with Elephants and Buffaloes, but though I several times searched for them, my labour was in vain, neither my people nor myself discovering any thing; indeed I saw once the print of an Elephant's foot, though almost effaced, from which I conjectured that if chance should sometimes bring one of those animals into this neighbourhood, the inhabitants pursue and oblige it (when they cannot succeed in killing it) to gain the more distant parts.

CHAP.

CHAP. IX.

THE AUTHOR CROSSES THE RIVER KLEIN-BRAK—DESCRIPTION OF THE COUNTRY OF AUTENIQUAS—POLITELY RECEIVED BY MR. MULDER—SHOOTS A TOURACO—FALLS INTO A PITT.

ON the seventh, at five o'clock in the morning, I left Muscle Bay, and at one o'clock crossed the river called *Klein-Brak*, which rises in a wood behind the chain of mountains at about a league from the sea. The next day we reached the great river of the same name, which is only three leagues farther; the tide flows a considerable way up, and renders its water brackish. We were obliged to wait 'till the ebb, in order to cross without danger. In this interval I shot several Pelicans, and Phœnicopteres, or Flamingoes, which were in great abundance; the deep red of the one, contrasted with the extreme whiteness of the other, produces a very pleasing affect on the eye.

In quitting the river we had a very steep mountain to ascend, the sight of it somewhat alarmed me, but patience, care and time, brought us to the summit, when we were well recompensed for our fatigue by a beautiful prospect that presented itself to our view, of one of the finest countries in the world. Eastward the vast chain of mountains, covered with forests, bounded the prospect; underneath an immense valley, that extended to the sea shore, interspersed sperfed with little hillocks of various forms; the excellent pastures, enameled with flowers, added a heightening to the scene, which gave me infinite delight. This country bears the name of *Auteniquas*, which in the Hottentot language signifies a man loaded with honey; in effect you cannot walk a step without meeting with swarms of bees. The earth is covered with flowers, whose mingled perfumes delight the smell, and invite you to loiter in this charming spot, where every beauty that imagination ever gave to fairy-land seems realised! The bells of almost all these flowers are impregnated with the ambrosial dews from which the bees collect their honey; this they deposit in hollow trees, or in the crevices of rocks. My people wished to remain in this delightful place, but fearing it might prove another Capua, I gave orders to continue our march towards the river *Wet-Els*, which takes its name from the woods that shade the banks; we had

now

now travelled seven leagues from the river Klein-Brak.

On the ninth we crossed several small rivulets that run from the mountains to the sea, these waters have the colour of Madeira, and taste of iron. Does this colour and taste proceed from some mine which they pass through, or from the roots and leaves they wash away and bring with them? I did not give myself time to unravel this mystery. We were near the last post maintained by the Company, which we gained after three hours hard travel.

I was now about to bid adieu to every vestige of human government, and mingle with those beings who live in a state of nature.

Mr. Mulder, the commander, came to receive me with great friendship; he has under him an inferior officer and fifteen men,

men, who have all been foldiers or failors in the company's fervice: Thefe cut wood for its ufe, and conftruct the waggons which convey it to the Cape. This is a moft ridiculous contrivance; for, was the wood conveyed to Mufcle-bay, one fmall bark would tranfport in a fingle voyage, as much as they carry, in the ufual manner, in three years, which would certainly be a confiderable faving to the company, and of general utility to the colonies, as well as to the inhabitants of Cape-Town, who would not then be neceffitated to burn only brufh faggots, which are gathered at great expence in the neighbourhood, by flaves kept for that purpofe; and coft at leaft double the price of the beft wood that can be procured in Paris.

Would any one believe, that the India directors fend every year, from Amfterdam, feveral fhips loaded with plank of all kinds,

kinds, a paffage of more than two thoufand leagues, into a country abounding with immenfe forefts of the fineft timber in the world? But this is accounted for, when we are informed that the company furnifhes the governor and officers with all the wood they want, delivered at their habitations clear of expence; fo that they have no perfonal intereft that can engage them to extend their views of adminiftration fo far; or to deftroy an abufe, which is contrary to the eafe and intereft of the colonies.

All the country of *Auteniquas*, from the mountains to the fea, is inhabited by colonifts, who breed vaft quantities of cattle, make butter, gather honey, and cut wood, all which articles are fent to the Cape. I was almoft exafperated to fee thefe people, who have fuch plenty of timber at hand, difpofe of all they could cut, not building themfelves tenable houfes, but living in mife-

miserable huts, formed of hurdles, covered with earth. The skin of a buffalo, tied by the corners to four stakes, serves as a bed; a mat closes the entrance, which is also the window; two or three broken chairs, some pieces of plank by way of table, and a miserable box of about two feet square compose the whole furniture of one of these dens. The extreme misery of the dwellings disagreeably contrasts the charms of this terrestrial paradise, whose beauties extend beyond the limits of *Auteniquas*. In other respects these people live luxuriously; they have plenty of game and sea-fish, and enjoy an advantage over the other colonists, in having, all the year, without interruption, their gardens well stocked with vegetables.

They owe these advantages both to the goodness of the soil, and the natural waterings from the various rivulets that wind and cross each other in a thousand different direc-

directions; and lay under contribution (if I may so express myself) the four seasons of the year.

These streams, which are never dry, have their source in the high western mountains, which being covered with immense forests, stop and collect the fogs and mists that are brought over them by the east winds from the sea, and occasion frequent rains.

It being convenient for me to remain some days with the commander, I broke in upon my established plan; for besides the polite reasons I had for waiting on him, his civility and friendship were expressed with such warmth, that I could not possibly excuse myself; and perhaps he received some pleasure, by reflecting on the character of kindness and hospitality, which in justice I could not fail to render him, on my return to the Cape.

I con-

I continued, according to my ufual cuftom, to furvey the country; in the woods I found the prints of buffalos and elephants feet, which appeared frefh made. I alfo faw a number of different birds, which were unknown to me, particularly the *Touraco*; fo many incentives were not neceffary to detain me in the neighbourhood of this place; efpecially, as at four or five leagues diftance from Mr. Mulder's, I found, on the fkirts of a foreft, a fituation very convenient for my camp.

Mr. Mulder was preparing to depart for the Cape; he furnifhed me with twenty pounds of gun-powder; and I profited by this occafion to write to my friends, and remit to Mr. Boers, a hundred curious birds and a box of infects. I likewife made an addition to my team of oxen, engaged three more Hottentots, and purchafed a young horfe, which I intended to break for hunting.

On

On the 9th of February I took leave of Mr. and Madam Mulder, with design to take possession of the great forest, and encamp on the spot which I had already chosen.

I had sent part of my people before me, to cut down some trees, clear away the brambles, and make some other necessary preparations for pitching my tent, which were carefully executed.

Our kitchen was placed under a great tree, which was very convenient for that purpose; my Hottentots arranged every thing in the best manner in their power, and constructed themselves some huts. At about ten paces from us was a limpid stream, and at a little distance a gentle hill, covered with grass, for our cattle; who, finding plenty of pasture, were sure to be always at hand. Many conveniences rendered this halt agreeable; but we were several times obliged to change our situation, in quest of game; which, frighted by the frequent firing, became scarce, and would have entirely abandoned us.

I was sometimes visited by the inhabitants of this district, by which means I readily procured fruits, vegetables, milk, and whatever they could supply me with; to say the truth, their visits cost me some bottles of brandy; but as I was not fond of spirits, and never partook of them, except as a cordial, my reserve in that respect kept them within bounds, and the wounds given to my casks were not very deep.

I well knew, that in the wood where I had fixed my camp, I might procure some *Touracos*; I was totally unacquainted with these birds, but was determined to go in quest of one. I soon perceived some, which I pursued in vain, for they always
perch

perch on the extremities of the higheft branches, and were never within reach of my gun. One day, after dinner, I purfued one with great eagernefs; he was hopping from bough to bough, and feemed to mock my efforts for a whole hour; in this time I had followed him a confiderable way; impatient at not being able to get near him, I fired at random, and at laft had the fatisfaction to fee him fall. My joy was inexpreffible; but the worft was to come, as I had yet to find my prize. I remarked the place where he fell, and ran among the brambles to pick it up; in my efforts to arrive at the fpot, I violently tore my hands and legs, but my fearch was in vain; I examined every bufh, I beat the fame thicket twenty times over, all my cares were ufelefs; the *Touraco* was no where to be found.

On reflection I concluded that I had only broken one of its wings, which might

might not prevent its getting a confiderable way from the place where it fell; I therefore went further on, continuing my fearch for more than half an hour; ftill no *Touraco* was to be feen. I was in difpair; the thorns and briars, which had torn even to my face, added to the vexation of lofing my bird, agitated me in a manner difficult to be defcribed; and, in that moment, nothing lefs than a lion or tiger to purfue, could have glutted my rage. A pitiful bird—after fo much pains and trouble— even after I had fhot it to difappear!—— I ftamped with my feet, and ftruck the ground with my gun——on a fudden it gave way, and I difappeared myfelf, falling into a pit twelve feet deep! Aftonifhment, and the pain occafioned by my fall, took place of anger. I found myfelf at the bottom of one of thofe covered fnares which the Hottentots dig for wild beafts, and particularly for the elephant.

When

When I had a little recovered from my fright, I began to think of the means of extricating myself; and was happy to find I was not impaled on the pointed ftakes which they fix at the bottom; happier yet, that I had not met with company, which might, however, every moment arrive, particularly if I was obliged to remain there the whole night; the approach of which began to deprefs me with terror and confternation, as it would prevent my ufing the only means in my power to extricate myfelf from this fatal place, without affiftance. My plan was to dig an afcent on one fide, with my hanger; but this would require much time in the performance; I therefore took the refolution to charge my gun, which I continued firing as often as poffible, hoping I fhould be heard at my camp. From time to time I liftened, palpitating with impatience; prefently I heard the report of two pieces, which gave me inexpreffible joy.

I made no doubt but my people were seeking me, and continued firing by intervals, to direct them to the spot. They soon arrived, well armed, and in the greatest consternation; for they entertained no doubt but I was pursued by some wild beast; instead of which they found me caught, like a fox, in a trap.

My men immediately cut a large bough and put it down into the pit, by means of which I soon clambered out. This escape, which I thought almost as great a deliverance as the prophet Daniel's, did not make me forget the *Touraco*; my dogs had followed the Hottentots, and I thought I should be able, by their aid, to discover it. I was not disappointed; they found him in a thicket of brambles, and the pleasure I felt at having this charming bird in my possession, made me forget the pain and danger it had occasioned.

I found

I found in his craw a kind of fruit which they are particularly fond of, and it was to thofe trees I afterwards reforted, either when I wifhed to fhoot, or fpread fnares to take them alive; and, by both thefe means, procured as many as I pleafed.

This bird is as agreeable in its form and plumage, as in the fweetnefs and melody of its notes; it is of a bright green, a tuft of the fame colour, bordered with white, adorns its head; its eyes a bright red, with a ftreak over them of the moft dazzling white; its wings are a beautiful purple, varying to the violet, according to the point of light in which it is viewed.

Thofe naturalifts who have reckoned it a fpecies of the cuckow have been guilty of a miftake; for it has not the leaft affinity with them.

In every part of the world, the cuckow fubfifts on fnails, and infects; but the *Touraco* is frugivorous.

In whatever climate the cuckow may be, 'tis remarkable, that fhe never builds a neft, but lays her eggs in thofe of other birds, and by this means efcapes the trouble of rearing her young; while the *Touraco*, on the contrary, is careful of its family, builds a neft, and hatches her own eggs.

This difference in their difpofitions is, I think, a fufficient reafon to prove them a particular fpecies. But I fhall fpeak more of it in my Ornithology.

CHAP.

ACCOUNT OF A NEW MODE OF SHOOTING—EX-
TRAORDINARY RAINS—GREATLY DISTRESS-
ED FOR FOOD—ARRIVES AT PAMPOEN-KRAAL
—DESCRIPTION OF IT—FISHING PARTY—
IN DANGER FROM A BUFFALO.

WHEN rains, or unbearable heats, interrupted my researches, I was not idle, but employed those intervals, which were not frequent, in my tent, making traps and snares to take different kinds of birds and animals alive; but it will hardly be believed, that I contrived to obtain the smallest and most delicate birds

birds with my gun, in a lefs injured ftate than I could procure them by any other means.

It may not be amifs for the fake of naturalifts, who, like me, take pains to gather a collection of birds, &c. to mention the method I *invented*. I run no hazard in making ufe of this expreffion, as I believe no other perfon ever had an idea of it.———Having charged my gun with fuch a quantity of powder as I thought, according to the fize or diftance of the bird, would anfwer the purpofe, I ran over it a layer of melted tallow, about half an inch in thicknefs, and preffed all clofe with my ram-rod; I then filled up the barrel of the piece with water, and, when at a proper diftance from the game, difcharged its contents, which only ftuned and wet his wings. This never failed to bring him to the ground, and give me an opportunity of picking it up before it had

In my firſt experiments, when I have been too near, or had charged with too much powder, or more fat than was neceſſary, I have found it intire in the body of the bird; but by a little practice, I learned how to adjuſt the requiſite proportions in ſuch a manner as ſeldom to fail of ſucceſs. I ſuppoſe it is unneceſſary to add, that the game muſt be conſiderably above you, ſince one may eaſily divine, that when charged in this manner, it is impoſſible to fire in a horizontal direction.

Since

Since my return to Europe, being one day at a friend's houſe in the country, ſome in company, who were totally unknown to me, were ſpeaking of the method I have juſt deſcribed; one among them, in oppoſition to the reſt, maintained by very ſpecious arguments, that my account muſt be, at leaſt, greatly exaggerated.

While they were diſputing I withdrew, and having prepared a fowling-piece, preſented myſelf before a window that overlooked the garden; the gentlemen were ſtill arguing; I made them obſerve a ſmall bird that was perched on the bough of a tree; I ſhot at it—it fell—and I had the ſatisfaction of delivering it alive into the hands of the reaſoner, who was now compleatly ſilenced.

Towards the end of the month we could not continue our journey, for the prodigious and almoſt inceſſant rains that fell;

fell; the thunder broke several times in the forest, very near our camp. The waters insensibly gained upon us from all parts; and, to complete our misfortunes, in one night we were intirely overflowed. We left the wood, and pitched our tent in a more elevated situation; but I saw with grief and concern, that it would be impossible to quit this place.

Those little rivulets that lately appeared so beautiful, were changed into furious torrents, which bore away sands, trees, and even pieces of rock; I saw it would be impossible to cross them without provoking the most imminent danger; to add to our disasters, the oxen left our camp, nor did I know which way to send after, or how to regain them.

My situation was truly alarming, and occasioned me some very uneasy hours; the Hottentots, worn out with fatigue,

began

began to murmur; our food began to be very scarce, not being able to shoot any game, or at least so small a quantity, that it was barely sufficient to support us; and to render our misfortunes complete, we could procure no assistance from the neighbouring colonists.

What an afflicting moment! this sudden inundation seemed to threaten Africa with another deluge. I endeavoured, however, to conceal part of my alarms from my melancholy companions, in whose looks of silent sorrow, fear was strongly painted.

Never was a greater alteration in so short a time; our charming walks were destroyed, and rendered desolate, by the rushing waters; the smiling face of the country was changed to an uninhabitable and gloomy desart! In this distress I summoned up all my resolution, intreated my
people

people to seek for our dispersed cattle, being determined to risk crossing one of the torrents, whatever might be the consequence. This attempt, which seemed to threaten inevitable destruction, was in a great measure the means of our preservation; for one of my Hottentots, in pursuance of this design, seeking for the safest passage to cross at, perceived a Buffalo in the water, which from the freshness of its appearance, might probably have been drowned the preceding night.

He returned with exclamations of joy to inform us of this happy news; indeed nothing could have been more welcome, as we were reduced to the greatest extremity for want of food. With some danger we dragged the animal to shore; he was cut up on the spot; the principal part being carried to my tent, the dogs (who had long fasted, and were reduced to moveing skeletons) found in what we left behind

hind sufficient to satisfy their hunger, and returned home with extended sides.

In this world nothing is permanent! Misfortunes terminate as well as pleasures! The end of March brought change of weather, the rains were neither so frequent nor so violent, consequently the torrents were considerably sunk, and abated much of their rapidity. I sent four of my Hottentots to seek our oxen, who after some days absence returned with the major part of them; some were found returning back to my camp, who, it was supposed, had wandered as far as the great river *Saumache*; others had taken refuge in different plantations, the rest sheltering themselves in the best manner they could: In short, four only were missing, these my people could not find, nor did I ever gain any intelligence of them.

I prepared without delay to quit this unlucky spot, intending to pitch my tent on a hill at about three leagues distance, called *Pampoen Kraal*, I took advantage of two fine days, to dry my effects, which were much injured by the weather; and the skin of the Buffalo was of great use in repairing the damage the traces of our waggons had sustained. In the midst of these incessant rains and my uncomfortable reflections, I had been capable of some exertion: In the wood I discovered an old hollow tree, whose trunk secured me from the inclemency of the weather, here I sat the greatest part of the day watching for game, and shooting all that came within my reach; our wants had not extinguished my curiosity: a perpetual wish to acquire these natural treasures overbalanced every other consideration, and though fainting with hunger I was eager to augment my collection.

Spite of every impediment, I had preserved a number of objects unknown in Europe. I had the satisfaction to see my riches daily increase, having taken such precautions, that the water had not injured them.

We found no game of the deer kind in this wood, except the *Gazell Bosbock*, and another species rather smaller, which I have mentioned in passing the *Duiven Ochs*.

The plain (in addition to three sorts of partridges I have already specified) abounds in a bird called the *Red Pheasant*, its feet and breast, which are bare, being of that colour.

There are plenty of Hyænas and Tygers about this place, but no lions.

The serene weather and beautiful aspect of the sky, seemed now to promise us a recompense

recompense for our former cruel situation. The hill of *Pampoen Kraal*, where I had pitched my tent, pleased me extremely. At a little distance from it was an eminence covered with a thicket of thirty or forty feet diameter, whose trees and bushes were so interwoven with each other, that the whole seemed of one growth. I determined to make this my residence, and in pursuance of this design, had an opening of about seven feet high, and sufficiently wide to afford an easy passage, cleared to the center; here, by the help of our hatchets, we formed two compleat squares, in one of which I placed a table and chair, and named it my *Workshop*, the other I adorned with the kitchen utensils, and reckoned it my dining-room.

These recesses, naturally roofed with branches and leaves to an impenetrable thickness, were to me a most charming and refreshing retirement! Here, after the morning's morning's chafe, when covered with duft and oppreffed with heat, I would fhelter myfelf from the mid-day fun; when fatigue had fharpened the appetite, how excellent was the repaft! When thought ftole on, how pleafing were my contemplations! or, if furprifed by fleep, how gentle, how peaceful, were my flumbers!

Sumptuous grottos of our wealthy financers, magnificent villas of Englifh citizens, nabobs and plunderers, what are your purling ftreams, your cafcades, your artificial mounts, zig-zag walks, bridges, ftatues, or all thofe objects which flatten on the fenfe, and fatigue the eye——what are ye when compared to the fimple unaffected beauties of *Pampoen Kraal!*

Though loath to leave this charming folitude, I began to prepare for my departure. One day, while I was viewing the environs, and obferving which road

we

Ca-Kraal

morning's chafe, when covered with duft and oppreffed with heat, I would fhelter myfelf from the mid-day fun; when fatigue had fharpened the appetite, how excellent was the repaft! When thought ftole on, how pleafing were my contemplations! or, if furprifed by fleep, how gentle, how peaceful, were my flumbers!

Sumptuous grottos of our wealthy financers, magnificent villas of Englifh citizens, nabobs and plunderers, what are your purling ftreams, your cafcades, your artificial mounts, zig-zag walks, bridges, ftatues, or all thofe objects which flatten on the fenfe, and fatigue the eye——what are ye when compared to the fimple unaffected beauties of *Pampoen Kraal!*

Though loath to leave this charming folitude, I began to prepare for my departure. One day, while I was viewing the environs, and obferving which road

we

A View of the Camp at Pampoen-Kraal

we might take with the greatest safety, I discovered at about a league distance from my camp, a very rapid torrent, which is called *Le trou de Kayman* (Cayman's hole) though I do not know why, for I never saw either Crocodile, or Aligator in this country.

The torrent rushes between two mountains, which are not very high, but excessive steep; on my right hand at about the distance of a thousand paces, was the sea; on the left woods and mountains, impassable for our beasts and carriages, and to attempt the dangerous passage of Cayman's hole, was my only resource. I was uneasy, even chagrined, to be thus obstructed at every step, and to find I had no sooner conquered one obstacle, than another started up.

Powerful as were my inclinations to proceed, the torrent was too much swelled by by the late rains to admit even a possibility of passing it with safety; I feared for my cattle more than for my effects, which we might have contrived to carry over on rafts. In this predicament I had only to wait with patience till the water should be abated.

On the eighteenth of April I received an express from Mr. Mulder, who had returned from the Cape, and brought answers to those letters he had conveyed for me in the beginning of February. Some of my friends, uneasy at my situation, intreated me to return; others, on the contrary, urged me to perseverance, and safe by their own fire sides, thought slightly of all obstacles, provided my travels might tend to the improvement of human understanding; or perhaps, without extending their views so far, would have been content if they only furnished food to satisfy their curiosity.

I determined, however, to continue the journey according to my original plan, though the bad weather had greatly retarded it, having only proceeded eight leagues, in the time Mr. Mulder had been to the Cape and back again. Among the rest I had a letter from him, in which he proposed meeting me for the purpose of a sea-fishing, provided it would not derange me too much. He informed me, he should bring nets and every convenience for a fortnight's residence on the shore; adding his wife would grace this little fête with her presence.

The news gave me pleasure; my friends were not long after their messenger, Mr. Mulder bringing the second commandant with him. The whole company was on horseback, it appeared like the travels of the Patriarchs; Mr. Mulder carrying a child of four months old before him, which his wife suckled; his waggons with the nets

nets and other necessaries were sent to the sea shore.

I caused one of mine to be prepared, and loaded with a tent and some empty casks, which I thought might be serviceable in our fishery. When arrived at a part of the coast which appeared favourable for our purpose, we cast our nets several times but with very indifferent success, taking scarce any thing; this determined us to go farther on to a small lake, which is formed by the spring tides, where we hoped we should meet with better sport. For my own part, I would much rather have been in quest of birds than fish, and it was more the friendship I felt for Mr. Mulder, with the chearful gaiety of the ladies, than any pleasure I expected to find in fishing, that made me of the party; and notwithstanding all those attractions, I frequently rambled about in search of my favorite amusement.

We

We had but just arrived on the borders of the lake, and pitched on a convenient place for erecting our tents, when we were near having our whole plan of opperations deranged; for in cutting a quantity of rushes which were very tall and thick, the workmen suddenly stumbled on a Buffalo, that was concealed among them; the animal was as much frightened as the men, and rushing hastily out, overturned the horses belonging to the second commandant and his wife; the alarm became general, every one making the best use of his legs. Mr. Mulder's domestics, who were unused to Buffalos, being near the water, rushed into it up to their chins; but my people, who were more accustomed to them, put a tolerable face on the matter.

The animal, confounded at the sight of such a company, not knowing which way to escape, stood scared and motionless in a nook of the rock; unhappily, I had

had only my double barrelled gun with me, and it could not be supposed that a common ball stood much chance of killing buffalo. I drew as near him as I dared, and fired one of my charges; at first he ran furio*sly towards* me, but my second shot taking effect, intimidated him; when turning aside, he discharged all his fury on an unfortunate ox that carried part of our provisions, and striking the peaceful animal twice in the belly with his horns, rushed by, and we lost sight of him.

The company could not be persuaded to remain on this spot; the husbands were apprehensive on their wives account; and, if I did not judge amiss, were not intirely without fear on their own; we resolved, therefore, to return to our former situation.

Fortune

Fortune was now favourable, and we had the satisfaction to take such quantities of fish, that I ordered my men to salt and fill my barrels with them. Mr. Mulder followed my example. Our sport lasted eight days; employing and amusing us more than I had expected. During this time, as I hinted before, I made some little excursions, in which I shot several curious birds; but met with no more buffalos.

When our fish were salted we divided them, each taking his share. I could not, without regret, part with these honest colonists, who had made our fishery pleasing, by the ingenuous and frank simplicity of their manners. I followed, with my eyes, their little caravan; nor did I turn away, 'till I had lost sight of them.

When I got back to my camp, I found every thing in order, and the beasts in good condition, for which I did not fail to testify

testify my satisfaction. I had put into the hands of Mr. Mulder, for the purpose of being remitted to Mr. Boers, at the Cape, all the birds I had prepared since my last parcel; with these I sent a living Touraco, which I had caught in a snare. Mr. Mulder was likewise so obliging as to give me one of his nets, and send me a pair of wheels, which he knew I was in great want of.

My cart was very inconvenient, and in continual danger of overturning; I had determined, on the first opportunity, to have two wheels added to it; this was a matter of necessity, and we set about making the alteration on the spot, every one putting a hand to the work. The wood requisite for this business was presently cut out, and, in less than a fortnight, my cart was transformed into a four wheeled waggon. This had not, I must confess, a very workman-like appearance, but

but it answered my purpose tolerably well.

This interval was not intirely devoted to one object; when my cartwrights had got what materials they wanted, and I had reason to think the work would be finished to my satisfaction, I employed a part of my people in repairing the roads, and filling up the ravines, occasioned by the floods, between us and the torrent we had to cross; I made them cut down a great number of large branches from the trees, and collect a quantity of stones for that purpose; and, had I not taken this precaution, I should have endangered, if not disabled, the carriages.

On the 13th of April, my caravan being in readiness to pursue the journey, I cast a last look on the delightful hermitage of *Pampoen Kraal*, and quitted it with as much reluctance as a lover does his mistress

tress. I have often since enquired after that charming asylum, and have heard, with satisfaction, that the Hottentots continue to respect, and have named it after me.

CHAP. XI.

AN ACCIDENT HAPPENS TO ONE OF THE WAGGONS — THE AUTHOR IS TAKEN ILL — RECOVERS — PURSUES HIS JOURNEY — ACCOUNT OF THE BUFFALO — HINTS RESPECTING THE BAY OF AGOA.

NOTWITHSTANDING all my precautions, we found great difficulty in passing Cayman's-hole, and likewise likewife a river, which the Hottentots, in their language, call *Krakede-kau*, which fignifies *Maid's-ford*.

This country was formerly inhabited by Hottentots, who have been either deftroyed or difperfed into other parts; the large pits we often met with, announced them to have been huntfmen, who caught in thefe fnares elephants, buffalos, &c. which are not now to be found in this quarter.

After eight hours march, we arrived at the *Swart-rivier*, (Black-river) which was yet overflowed in confequence of the late rains; we were obliged to crofs it upon rafts, conftructed in the fame manner as thofe we had before made ufe of.

Difcovering fome traces of buffalos feet on the other fide; I refolved to ftop there, and

and had the satisfaction to kill one myself, and the Hottentots who attended me another. We returned in haste to the camp, to inform them of our succefs, thefe being fufficient to fupply us with provifion for a confiderable time, in cafe we did not happen to meet with frefh.

We encountered thefe two buffalos on the banks of a river that flowed from a hill above our fettlement; by my orders they were pufhed into the ftream, which brought them down to my tent. I had thefe animals cut into fmall pieces, that they might the more readily imbibe the falt, and afterwards hung to dry in the air. The bufhes, branches of trees, our waggons, in fhort, every thing that furrounded us was occupied with pieces of buffalo. In the height of our bufinefs we had fome unexpected and unwelcome vifitants, being affailed by a flight of kites, vultures, and other birds of prey, who came

came among us without any sign of fear; the kites, particularly, were so bold as to snatch the meat from my men, fly to the neighbouring trees, and devour it before our eyes. I fired at them several times, but this did not prevent the return of others; I therefore resolved to adopt other measures, and while our provision was drying, drive them away with long switches. This method was very fatiguing to my men, who, maugre all their care, were very much plundered; but had we omitted this precaution, not a single piece of our two buffalos would have remained.

I had the tongues smoaked, and was so well pleased with them, that whenever I met with any, I never failed to have them prepared in this manner; but I never fancied the tongues of the elephants, there was a something in the taste, and even in the form, that occasioned a disgust I could neither overcome or account for.

Having well dried and packed our provisions, we abandoned Black-river. At two leagues distance we crossed the *Gaucom*, and after travelling the same space reached the *Nysena*, which was very considerable, and augmented by the tide. I had never seen a more agreeable spot for my camp; it was a beautiful meadow, about a thousand feet square; a forest of large trees on the south formed a magnificent curtain that extended to the west; on the north was the river, which appeared to contain plenty of fish, while a variety of game sported on the borders; so many advantages might almost have made me forget Pampoen-Kraal, yet I was not tempted to stop.

On the opposite side of the river was a high mountain, this we must necessarily pass;

pass; but it appeared so steep and dangerous, that it gave me much inquietude, lest some accident should happen. These fears were very near being verified, by the loss of all the fruit of my labour and fatigue.

I had the precaution only to take one of my waggons up at a time; indeed, had I wished to have them go together I had not oxen enough to draw them.

I had twenty put to the master waggon, which contained, as I have before observed, all my artillery and acquisitions. The oxen began ascending the hill; they drew with their utmost strength; they strained every nerve, and had almost reached the summit, when the chain that held the first eighteen broke, and the waggon ran, or rather rolled back, with dreadful precipitation, draging with it the remaining two that were fastened to the shafts.

shafts. From the height we had gained, myself and Hottentots beheld the disaster with anxious and palpitating hearts. Twenty times was it on the brink of a precipice which was on one side of the road; and this misfortune must infallibly have happened, had it not been for the amazing strength of the remaining oxen. In this case I must have relinquished the journey, as my waggon, arms and most valuable effects would have been broke into a thousand pieces.

The waggon had almost gained the river, when it was fortunately stopped by the projection of a rock; a circumstance that caused us to hasten down with exclamations of joy.

After replacing every thing in the best order, we harnessed our cattle once more, and in about an hour regained, without any

any further danger, what we had loft in ten minutes.

The other not being fo heavy, was got up without much difficulty; but I now took the precaution to double the traces, and place a man at each wheel, ready to lock them on the fmalleft appearance of danger; for though the road was fo fteep that this would not have prevented their defcent (fuppofing we had met with a fimilar accident) it would greatly retard the rapidity, and give us time to direct and keep them from the precipice.

Fear magnifies every appearance of danger; I had dreaded the worft, and vainly endeavoured to tranquilize my countenance during the agitation of my mind. In that terrible moment I eagerly followed the track of the waggon, each jolt being a fhock to my heart.

On recollection, I thought we got off very cheaply; indeed, it seemed almost a miracle that no material injury should be done to the waggon; and what was still more surprising, my two oxen, dragged backward by a carriage of between four and five thousand pounds weight, who might have been dashed to pieces before they could have reached the foot of the mountain, got clear for some trifling wounds that did not by any means disable them.

As I got farther from the colonies the country was still more beautiful; the soil rich and fruitful. Here nature appeared in all her majesty; the lofty mountains offering from every side the most delightful and romantic views I had ever seen: This prospect contrasted with the idea of the parched and barren sands about the Cape, made me think myself at a thousand miles distance.

" What !"

"What!" exclaimed I, "shall these charming fields, these hills and valleys, be for ever uninhabited, except by the lion and the tiger! What a being is the sordid speculator, whose views, bounded by commerce, port-fees and customs, can prefer the storms and dangers of Table-bay, to the safe riding, or natural and charming ports, that are so common on the oriental coasts of Africa!"

It was thus I ruminated while walking up the mountain; entertaining myself with the idea of this beautiful country's being peopled, and forming schemes which the political laziness of the Europeans will never execute.

We continued our journey, having still to the west the great chain of mountains covered with forests; and after four hours and a half's march stopped at a little rivulet, about three leagues distant from the sea.

fea. We obferved that a prodigious quantity of fifh came up with the tide; when at its height I caufed the ftream to be barred with Mr. Mulder's large net, which I now ufed for the firft time, doubling it, as it would otherwife have been too large.

I might be thought to exaggerate, was I to mention the number of fifh we caught on the ebbing of the tide; the quantity was fo great as to damage the net confiderably. My men dreffed them according to their fancy, I referved a hundred for my own ufe, which I put into a pot with fome fpices, without water, clofing the top with clay, and covering it over with hot embers; this arrangement procured me an excellent difh, which I eat of for feveral days.

It would be impoffible to chufe a more commodious and agreeable fituation, for

fettling

settling a prosperous colony, than this spot. The sea passing between two large rocks which are situated at about a thousand paces distance from each other, penetrates in-land for two leagues and a half, forming a spacious bason of a league in breadth; both sides are bordered with rocks, which cut off all communication with it, as far as they extend.

The soil is fertile, and intersected by numerous streams of fresh water from the western mountains, whose beautiful woods by various turnings and windings, extend even to the bason, and present the delighted eye with a hundred natural and charming groves.

On the borders I found several small white Herons, of the same species as those sent from Cayenne, and which I had seen in my youth at Surinam. I also saw the large white Egret, or Heron, but it is very scarce.

The woods abound with game, have plenty of Buffalos and some Elephants. At considerable distances from each other are scattered some miserable habitations, whose owners are reduced to subsist on a precarious commerce of wood and butter to the Cape.

I remained in this country 'till the thirteenth, we then crossed by dreadful roads a forest called *Le Poort*, from thence in seven hours we reached the *Witte Drift*; I saw in different places some plantations, like those I last mentioned, the distance, and many other almost insurmountable difficulties seldom permit them to take their cattle to the Cape, and when this is accomplished, they are generally in so poor a state, that they are obliged to sell them for half the usual value. On inquiry I found many of these Colonists had not been at the Cape for several years.

I still proceeded in my journey; but whether

whether the fatigues and difficulties I had lately encountered, or change of climate, had deranged my health, I was suddenly taken ill, and the gloomy idea seized me, that I should leave my ashes at two thousand leagues distance from my family.

Melancholy now painted my situation in all its horrors, and the deepest sadness preyed upon my spirits; I had a violent head-ach, with universal heaviness and pain, which made me apprehend the utmost danger; indeed ill health was the greatest misfortune I had dreaded in my enterprise. I was too much indisposed to pursue my journey, therefore resolved to continue where I was, convinced my illness would take the same turn here as in the midst of medical solemnity, and either terminate happily, or be concluded by death.

I visited the environs as well as my weak state of health would permit, and discovered

vered, in the neighbourhood of a little brook, a pleasing situation for our camp, my tent being placed on the skirts of a wood. Neither myself or people knew any thing of medicine, the only resource was diet and repose. My illness increased, and I was no longer able to quit the waggon, which the intense heat of the sun had converted into a kind of furnace. I was tormented with the most excruciating agonies in my bowels, the Hottentots were afflicted with similar complaints, which made me conclude we owed this disorder to the great quantity of salt fish we had eaten, and I immediately gave orders to burn all that remained.

A slow fever preyed upon me, but I had not entirely lost my strength, and after twelve days of violent perspiration began to recover, repose and diet seeming to produce the most salutary effects.

I now began to take a little moderate exercife, endeavoured to compofe my fpirits and found myfelf getting better every day, while the fame means re-eftablifhed the health of my Hottentots. I have ever fince entertained the higheft opinion of hot baths, and thought that which hazard (I might fay neceffity) adminiftered was the means of faving my life.

My health being perfectly recovered, I refumed my favourite occupation of hunting. In the firft excurfion I made for this purpofe, I found we were flanked by a fecond river, called *Queur-Boom*, which falls from the weftern mountains and joins *Witte Dreft*, a league before it reaches the fea, into which thefe waters empty themfelves by a mouth at the fide of a Bay, known to Navigators by the name of the Bay of Agoa.

In a journey that Governor Blettenberg (of the Cape) undertook to this part of the country, he caufed his name with the day and year of his arrival, to be engraven on a ftone column. I examined this whimfical monument, which only wanted an infcription in verfe to render it compleatly ridiculous; the name, however, has fpread throughout all the Colonies, and the Bay of Agoa is now only known by the appellation of *Blettenberg's Bay*. Thus it is that a paltry ftone, raifed by the vanity of an individual, may give birth to a number of errors, and difconcert eftablifhed information!

In this neighbourhood there was a troop of about twenty-five or thirty Bubales, in a fmall fpace inclofed by the fea and two rivers, whofe only entrance was occupied by the camp and waggons. The animals were entirely at our difcretion, not being able to efcape; indeed we looked on thefe as a part of our property, and when provisions grew short, did not fail to make use of them, I believe none escaped; their skins were joined together and formed an excellent tilt for our new waggon.

Considerable herds of Buffalos came and grazed within view on the other side of *Queur-Boom*, we sometimes hunted them and never failed of success. This animal is very shy, and in the woods should be attacked cautiously; but if in the open country, he is by no means formidable, being extremely timorous, and flying the presence of man. The best way to subdue him is to hunt him with some good dogs, and while the Buffalo is busily defending himself from their attack, a shot in the head, or near the shoulder-bone will usually stretch him dead upon the spot. The bullets used on this occasion should be cast in a larger mould than common, of a composition of lead and pewter. Unless the ball

ball lodges in one of the parts I have mentioned the wound is not mortal.

The horns of this animal are very large and divergent, being so near at the base, that they might be supposed to spring from the same root, and the points turning again towards each other, they seem to form a kind of chaplet.

The Buffalo is considerably larger and stronger than the finest European Ox, and I should suppose it is by no means impracticable to make it submit to the yoke. It may be objected, that every attempt at this has hereto failed; but I think the argument by no means conclusive. The enterprise requires time, address and information, therefore cannot be expected to succeed from the indolent attempt of an ignorant Colonist, who is apt to think every trifling difficulty insurmountable. The scheme is certainly worthy the speculation

culation of a company that wishes to extend and facilitate every branch of industry and commerce.

Let a number of these animals be procured while young, let them be secured in an inclosure, and accustomed to receive from their keeper the food they are most fond of, and I am persuaded they will soon be familiarized to the hand that feeds them. These animals will in time have young, who by the example of the old ones and the same mode of treatment, may be rendered still more sociable; and I see no reason to doubt but the third generation at farthest, would be tractable; while we, every day in Paris, see wolves taken from the uninhabited mountains of Savoy, walking about our streets, dancing, jumping and playing a hundred tricks, with all the submission that the caprice or interest of their conductors require.

In general the horned animals, who part the hoof, have a wildnefs in the eyes which makes them appear terrible, but it is not (as with carnivorous beafts) a fign of fiercenefs, on the contrary, it is an indication of fear; they have neither the craft or favagenefs of the Lion, Tiger, or even the Elephant, nor are the vegetables on which they feed fo conducive to a malignant difpofition.

It does not enter into my prefent plan to inveftigate the immenfe and complicate diftinctions which mark the different fpecies of favage animals; as thefe definitions have no relation with recitals which are purely hiftorical, I fhall leave them to my defcription of Quadrupeds; but I wifhed to obferve that it is ever a motive of defence, or neceffity of food that leads them to ferocity; governed by various combinations of the paffions, they take different means to gratify them.

I had not yet taken a view of the Bay, improperly called Blettenberg, indeed my illness had prevented it. On examination I was surprised to find it only an open road, which indents very little inland; it is spacious, and the largest ships may find good anchorage; shallops can easily gain a fine flat shore, which though not destitute of rocks, is not much incommoded by them, as they are at considerable distances from each other. About a league from the mouth of Queur-Boom the crews may take in plenty of fresh water, and procure refreshments from the inhabitants; the bay likewise abounds with fish, and the rocks are covered with excellent oysters.

This is one of the places where Government should establish a repository for timber, which is excellent in the environs, and much easier to obtain than in any other part I had seen. It does not grow like that in the country of *Auteniquas*, for instance, on the tops of high and steep mountains, but at hand, on the level plain, and were magazines constructed on the shore, one or two vessels might transport it to the Cape, in fine weather, in a short time; this would open the eyes of the inhabitants to the peculiar advantages of their situation, and the transportation of timber being considerably augmented, the cultivation of lands, cleared from these inexhaustible forests, would offer a flattering prospect of emolument to some intelligent colonists, who on account of the easy communication with the Cape, would have it in their power to obtain a number of indulgences they are forced to renounce, while it is necessary to take a journey of a hundred and fifty leagues by land to procure them. We should not then hear these good Hollanders openly and ardently wishing that some nation would settle in their neighbourhood, and furnish them with the conveniences of life and charms of society,

by

by extending the benefits of commerce to the Bay of Agoa; nor would these wishes, so contrary to their political consequence, run any hazard of being fulfilled.

It only remains for the company to form an establishment, which to public utility would add the profit of individuals; for example, felling the trees called *Bois-Puant*, (stinking wood) and transporting them to Europe, where they would certainly be accounted some of the finest for cabinet-work, would furnish an amazing profit.

The advantages the company and colonies might draw from this fine country, could never have escaped the observation of the Governor, who once visited it; but the truth is, public good is usually subordinate to the private advantages of some needy adventurers, who are interested to suppress every thing that tends to the diminution of their profits. What is a Governor?

vernor? An unfeeling being, blind to the general good, who is not stimulated, nor has any energy but for his own private advantage; who consents to exile himself from his native country for a time, and the first article of whose political creed is, that being rapidly to acquire a large fortune, every means tending to the accomplishment of his views, are good and lawful! Full of these ideas he departs for his government, arrives, realizes his designs, and returns to his country, to insult his fellow citizens, by an insolent display of that pride and riches, which must one day open the eyes of his superiors to means of redress, that could not fail to operate to the advantage and prosperity of a numerous colony. He is replaced by a successor, who enriches himself in his turn, and the farce is thus played a hundred times over.

I believe most Colonies that are the property of private companies, to be in the same

same predicament, with those public vehicles which convey merchandise and passengers from one place to another, where, provided the property does but get safe to the place of destination, we are not much concerned whether the wheels crack under the weight.

CHAP. XII.

KILLS A BALBUZARD — TAKES A GAZELL — PURSUES SOME ELEPHANTS — KILLS ONE — HIS LIFE ENDANGERED — REMARKABLE INSTANCE OF ATTACHMENT.

THE environs of this bay furnished me with an opportunity of adding several fine birds to my collection but above

above all I wished to procure one that had often put my patience to the proof, and in the sequel had like to have cost me dear; it was a beautiful kind of Balbuzard, which is a species of the eagle, and near as large as the osprey. I saw it every day about my camp, but never within reach of my gun; and I was always watching, or causing it to be watched.

One day that I had crossed *Queur-Boom*, and was walking along its opposite bank, I saw at the foot of an old withered tree, a number of fishes heads, with a quantity of bones and other remains of young gazells. I immediately concluded it was the common resort of the Balbuzard I had so often seen, and was confirmed in my conjectures when I saw two rising in the air to a prodigious heigth. I instantly concealed myself in a thick bush, but this was not sufficient to shield me from the piercing eyes of the eagles,

eagles, who, instead of descending, intirely disappeared.

The next morning I replaced myself in the thicket, which I never quitted till the evening, and then without having seen them return. Though this place was at no great distance from our camp, my jaunts were very troublesome; because in going and returning I had to cross *Queur-Boom*, and was frequently obliged to wait the ebbing of the tide.

Wearied with this loss of time; I ordered two of my Hottentots to follow me. We crossed the river, and got within gun-shot of the above-mentioned tree; here I made them dig a hole three feet square and four deep; into this pit I descended, causing a kind of hurdle made of crossed sticks, covered with a piece of mat, and then with earth, to be laid over the opening; in this there was a small aperture to look out at, or through which,

which, if occasion required, I could fire my piece. I then ordered my people to return to the camp. Day broke soon after, but the provoking birds did not appear, the earth being newly turned up, made them distrustful; indeed I had foreseen this difficulty, however I resolved to persevere in the plan I had adopted. In the evening I returned home, passed some hours at the camp, after which I crossed the river, and caused myself to be covered up as before. I passed the second day with no better success than the former; in this interval the sun had dried the earth which had been thrown up in making my hiding place. About twelve o'clock on the third day, I saw the female hovering over the tree, with a large fish in its beak; soon after it perched on one of the branches. I discharged my piece, which happily took effect, and she instantly fell, violently beating her wings. In a moment she renewed her flight, passed the river;

river; but dropped as foon as fhe had reached the oppofite fhore.

The joy I felt at feeing her lay motionlefs on the ground, made me regardlefs of the height of the tide; with my gun on my fhoulder, I rufhed into the river, nor was I fenfible of my folly 'till I found myfelf in the middle, and up to my chin in water.

I was alone, and totally unacquainted with fwimming; had I returned, the rapidity of the current would infallibly have overfet me, I therefore purfued my way, and had the good fortune to gain the other fide. I caught up the Balbuzard, and the pleafure I found in contemplating it, made me forget the danger I had juft encountered.

I haftened homeward; on my arrival I was informed that fome of my people were

were in pursuit of a buffalo, which they had seen by chance the evening before; they soon after returned, loaded with the quarters of the animal, having cut him up on the spot. Early the next morning I sent to collect all the offal that remained, purposing to lay it in a convenient place to attract the birds of prey; this method soon procured me a male Balbuzard, which does not differ from the female, except in being one-third smaller; a general case among all carnivorous birds.

One morning that I was seated at the opening of my tent, busily dissecting the Balbuzard I had killed the preceding day, on a sudden a gazell, of the kind called *Ros Bock*, crossed my camp, running with amazing swiftness between the waggons; my dogs who had seen it enter, had not time to prevent her escape; and though a net that was hung to dry on the tent interrupted her passage, she disengaged
herself

herself by instantly tearing away a part of it. My whole pack now began the pursuit; but with amazing celerity she gained the river side, and plunged into the stream.

There are a number of wild dogs in the neighbourhood of this place, nine of them (who had probably been in pursuit of her) appeared at this moment; but at sight of us they stopped short, and making a turn, gained a little hill beyond our camp, from whence they could perceive the pursuit of their prey, which my dogs had followed into the water, and were now draging alive to shore, in which state my Hottentots soon after brought her to the tent. It was laughable to see the silly disappointed look of these animals, who from fear never quitted the hill, and were only spectators of this scene. I would fain have caught one, and for that purpose sent some of my people to endeavour to bar their passage;

paſſage; but they were too cunning for us, eſcaping with the utmoſt ſpeed, and a ball I ſent after them was but thrown away.

I wiſhed to tame this gazell, but ſhe was ſo very timorous, ſtruggling and beating herſelf ſo violently at the ſight of my dogs, that I thought it more merciful to kill and eat her.

For eight days this adventure ſerved for matter of converſation and merriment among my facetious Hottentots, who were highly delighted at having ſnatched this prize from the mouths, as it were, of the before-mentioned hungry animals. If my dogs had not been ſeconded by the Hottentots, I make no doubt but the others would have carried off the gazell; for though my pack was more numerous, the wild ones were ſtronger and more courageous.——But I may have occaſion to speak

speak of them hereafter; when I shall contradict some errors which have been advanced respecting them, seemingly, with good authority. But how can matters be related with any degree of certainty, when the relator has never been witness to what he describes, but is reduced to the necessity of copying after those who knew as little of the matter as himself.

Until the 25th of June we frequently removed our camp to different parts adjoining the bay; I then resolved to continue my journey between the chain of mountains and the sea. I went to reconnoitre the passes, and determine which way we should proceed; but I found, to my inexpressible vexation, that there was no possibility of my waggons crossing the forest, which is of an amazing extent and thickness. My Hottentots, who had likewise been employed in the same manner, were not more fortunate; in a word, no path was to be difcovered. I now determined to crofs the chain of mountains in fearch of a road for the oxen, but my labour was ftill in vain; whatever fide I turned to, pointed rocks interfected my way, and offered infuperable obftacles to our paffage. I now found we had got in a fituation, fo befet on every fide with impaffible mountains, forefts, &c. that there was no way of quitting it but by the path we had entered; we were obliged, therefore, to return to the wood *Du Poort*, which we had left a month before.

Such is the happy pliability of the human mind, that the verieft trifles frequently calm our ruffled fpirits, and wipe off the remembrance of our misfortunes. This place, to which I regretted being forced to return, fuddenly gave me the greateft fatisfaction.

As

As I was walking along, I saw the print of an elephant's foot, so fresh that I was certain it could not be more than a day since it passed that spot; this circumstance immediately dissipated my regret, and consoled me for the delay of my journey. I gave orders, without loss of time, for my men to erect the tent.

Among my Hottentots there was one, who, in his youth, had visited this place with the Hoord to which he belonged; and though a long interval had elapsed, he yet retained some knowledge of the surrounding country. I selected him, therefore, with four of my best marksmen, for my elephant hunters, and ordering affairs at the camp, we took a small stock of provisions, and followed the track of the animal. Night coming on, we supped gaily, inviting each other by our chearfulness, not to regret the comforts of the camp; and after making a large fire,

fire, laid ourselves down to sleep upon the earth.

Though we had mutually endeavoured to inspire each other with confidence, a sentiment of uneasiness and terror pervaded the whole party, and the least wind, or rustling of the leaves, was sufficient to rouse and put us on our guard. The whole night passed away in these little agitations; and at day break I hastened up my companions, who were soon ready, a glass of brandy each making them forget their uneasy night and early rising, they followed me with the most pleasing alacrity.

The second day was not more fortunate; we pursued the same method as in the former, with this difference, that being a little emboldened by not having encountered any danger, we hoped to lose and forget our fatigues in sleep, which would enable us us to purfue our chace with redoubled ardor.

We had hardly been afleep an hour, when we were fuddenly alarmed by a buffalo, who, attracted by the light, had drawn very near us. This animal, who is much terrified at the fight of the human fpecies, no fooner perceived us, than he haftened away, and the noife he made in rufhing through the bufhes, had waked us; I immediately ran to my gun, but was too late, for the animal had fufficient time to efcape. We fought after him for more than an hour, and fired feveral fhot at random; but having no profpect of fuccefs, we again laid ourfelves down by the fire, and endeavoured to fleep.

The adventures of the third day became more interefting; I fhall be particular in my recital of them; they even now, frequently return upon my mind; and though the impetuosity of youth has given way to less animated projects and more tranquil ideas, the remembrance of this day, while it makes me tremble, gives to my mind a degree of animation.

We had not yet lost the traces of the animal we were in search of; after some hours fatigue and painful walking among the thorns and briars, we arrived at a very open part of the forest, in which was a clump of shrubs and under-wood. Here we stopped, while one of my Hottentots climbed a tree. After he had looked about for some time, he made a sign for us to be silent, by putting his finger on his mouth, and then, by opening and closing his hand several times (a signal we had before agreed upon) gave us to understand how many elephants he had discovered.

When

When he had defcended, we confulted what means to purfue; the refult of our deliberations was, that the perfon who had difcovered them, fhould lead us thro' the bufhes as near as poffible to the fpot where they ftood. Though he led me very near one of thefe enormous beafts, I did not at firft perceive him; not that fear had facinated my fight, but I could not believe that the prodigious immovable mafs beneath me was the animal I had fo much wifhed to encounter. It fhould be ob-ferved, I was on a little hillock, which raifed me above the back of the elephant, I ftill kept looking further on, and fhould rather have taken, what was fo near me, for a piece of rock than a living creature. All this time my honeft Hottentots kept crying, *fee there!—there he is!* with a tone of the utmoft impatience. At length a flight motion caught my eye, and im-mediately after the head and tufks, which the enormous body had in a manner con-cealed,

cealed, were turned towards me; without losing time or advantage in contemplation, I instantly fired my carbine, and the ball taking place in the middle of his forehead, he staggered and fell. This noise frighted the rest, and they immediately began running from the spot as fast as possible; they were about thirty in number, and it was really amusing to see their huge ears flapping in proportion to the quickness of their motions. This was but the prelude to a more animated scene.

I was examining the animal I had killed, when another passed just by us, which received a shot from one of my people; by the blood that followed the stroke, I judged he was dangerously wounded, and pursued him immediately. He would have lain down, but was prevented by our repeated firing. We followed him into a thicket, in which was a number of decayed trees, that had fallen through age.

On

On our fourteenth fire the animal became outrageous, making furiously after the Hottentot that last wounded him; another of my men discharged his piece, crying out, at the same time, " Take care of yourselves !" an injunction that every one immediately obeyed.

I was only at about twenty-five paces distance from the animal, with a gun of thirty pounds weight, besides ammunition, and not so conveniently situated for escape as my people, who had not advanced so far; I ran, but the elephant gained ground every moment. More dead than alive through fear; abandoned by the Hottentots (one of them only attempting to assist me) the only chance I had was to fall down by the trunk of a great tree that lay on the ground; this I had scarcely time to accomplish before the animal ran over it, but frighted himself at the noise made by my people, he instantly stopped to listen. I could

I could readily have fired from my hiding place, for fortunately my piece was charged; but he had already received so many wounds, that despairing to disable him by a single discharge, I remained immoveable, every moment expecting death. I continued, however, to watch him, resolving, if he discovered me, to sell my life as dear as possible.

The Hottentots trembling for my safety called out from all parts, but I took care not to answer; persuaded by my silence that I was already crushed to pieces, their cries redoubled.

The Elephant affrighted at this sudden clamour, turned hastily about, stepping a second time over the trunk of the tree, within six paces of where I lay, without perceiving me. Wishing to convince my Hottentots that I was living, and impatient at remaining in this perilous situation,

I

I got on my feet, when fending another ball after him, he continued his way and entirely difappeared.

This picture is not yet compleat, gratitude and friendſhip muſt cloſe the recital. Generous, worthy man! the hour is arrived in which I have ſo often promiſed to raiſe this artleſs monument to the commemoration of thy virtues; but thou canſt never know the eſtimation I ſet on it! Never can my euology pervade the peaceful boſom of thy defert; yet thou art not ignorant of my gratitude, the warmth of which I have ſometimes endeavoured to expreſs. Long wilt thou remember me, long ſhall I be ſpoken of among thy Hoord, and happier ſhall I be in that idea, than in all the uſeleſs trophies that could be beſtowed on me by the vanity of a poliſhed people! Generous ! *Klaas* pupil of nature! artleſs ſoul, undefaced, uncorrupted by the falſe tinfel of ſuperficial politeneſs, continue to
cheriſh

cherish the remembrance of that friend, to whom thy idea must ever be dear!

When in the above mentioned perilous situation, at the mercy of a furious animal, who once discovering, would have ended me in an instant; while my heart palpitated with apprehension, I was yet susceptible of a sentiment of veneration, inspired by one of those worthy men, whom polished nations have agreed to speak of with disdain, as the very out-casts of nature; in short, by an African savage! a Hottentot!

In quitting the Cape, *Klaas* had been recommended to me, by Mr. Boers, as a man whose courage and fidelity might be depended on; he ordered him never to abandon me, promising a recompense if I returned safe to the Cape, and gave a satisfactory account of his conduct; he faithfully obeyed these orders, never quitting me in the hour of danger, and in this instance

stance finding I had difappeared in an inftant, he fought me in vain; I could hear him call me with the utmoft emotion, and addrefs his comrades who followed at fome diftance, in terms of reproach for their cowardice. "What will you do," faid he, in his own expreffive language, "where can you go, fhould we have the misfortune to find our unfortunate mafter crufhed to pieces by the feet of the Elephant? Dare you return to the Cape without him? Have you the courage to face the Fifcal? Whatever excufe you may make, you will certainly pafs for his affaffins. But return to the camp, pillage his effects, do what you pleafe; for me, I am refolved to find my mafter, and if dead, to perifh with him." He accompanied this difcourfe with fuch lively expreffions of forrow, that in the moft critical moment my heart was fenfible of his attachment.

The report of my piece was an univerſal ſignal of joy; in a moment I was ſurrounded by my people. The affectionate *Klaas* knew no ſet terms in which to expreſs his ſatisfaction, but he preſſed me eagerly in his arms.

His comrades overcome with ſhame and regret, with ſupplicating faces ſeemed to aſk forgiveneſs. In few words I endeavoured to conſole them, enjoying this whole ſcene too much to interrupt the contemplation of it by idle ſpeeches or uſeleſs reproach.

From this time I experienced the ſatisfaction of being beloved without any mixture of intereſt. *Klaas* was now my equal, my brother, the confidant of my hopes and fears; more than once has he calmed my agitated mind, and re-animated my drooping courage; if in the ſequel he may ſhew ſome marks of weakneſs, inconſiſtent with
the

KLAAS,
The Author's favorite Hottentot.

the good order I had eftablifhed in my camp, the proofs of his attachment had too much weight to permit the exertion of feverity, or offering any impediments to the interefts of his heart.

I did not forget to draw a faithful refemblance of this worthy Hottentot, from which the annexed plate was engraved.

CHAP.

CHAP. XIII.

THE AUTHOR RETURNS TO THE CAMP — ATTACKS FOUR ELEPHANTS—RECEIVES A MESSENGER FROM MR. BOERS—WRITES TO HIS FRIENDS.

NIGHT drawing on, we haſtened to find the Elephant, which I had the good fortune to kill with a ſingle ſhot; our preſence drove away ſeveral Vultures and ſmall carnivorous animals, who had loſt no time, having already began to diſſect it.

The

The Hottentots quickly kindled several fires, provisions had began to run short, consequently this supply was very welcome to us; they cut several slices off the animal to broil for themselves, dressing a part of the trunk for me.

It was the first time I had tasted this kind of food, but I determined it should not be the last, as I thought it delicious. Klaas assured me the feet were still better, and promised to convince me of this by preparing a part of them for my next morning's breakfast, which operation he immediately set about.

Having cut off the Elephant's feet, they dug a hole in the earth, of three or four feet square, which was filled up with burning wood, covered over with dried branches, so as to keep a very brisk fire good part of the night. When they thought this pit sufficiently heated, the fire was
taken

taken out, and the four feet being placed in it, were covered over with warm afhes, then with lighted embers and fome fmall dry fticks, which continued burning 'till morning.

This night I was the only one that flept, my men keeping watch by order of Klaas. I was informed next morning that they had heard a number of Elephants and Buffalos all night in the environs; this indeed we had expected, knowing the foreft was full of them, but the number of our fires had prevented their giving us any difturbance.

My people prefented me with one of the before mentioned feet for breakfaft; drefsing had prodigioufly fwelled it, but it exhaled fuch a favory odour, that I foon tafted and found it to be delicious. I had often heard the feet of Bears commended, but could not conceive that fo grofs and
heavy

heavy an animal as the Elephant, would afford such delicate food. "Never," said I, "can our modern epicures have such a dainty at their tables; let forced fruits and the contributions of various countries contribute to their luxury, yet cannot they procure so excellent a dish as I have now before me."

The rest of the morning was employed in taking off the tusks, which did not weigh above twenty pounds, the animal being a female, and only eight feet three inches high. My men loaded themselves with as much provision as they could carry, and we returned towards the camp.

I had designed to follow the track of the beast we had wounded, but so many others had trampled about during the night, that it was impossible to discover the traces of it, and being all much fatigued, I feared

feared to dishearten my men, therefore determined to return as quick as possible.

How subtil a sense is sight in a Hottentot! which is seconded by a scrutinizing attention, almost miraculous! On a dry soil, where the Elephant, notwithstanding his weight, scarce leaves the smallest track; among a number of withered leaves, scattered by the wind, the African will trace his steps; a green leaf doubled or detached, the manner in which a small branch is broken off, with a thousand other circumstances equally minute, are to them certain informations, where all the resources of the most expert European hunter would be ineffectual. It was only by time and experience that I could form any idea of a kind of divination, so necessary in this noble species of hunting, which was so pleasing to me, that I was fond of the most trifling acquisition. While rambling in the woods with my people, the whole day

day was spent in questions and information, example being usually joined to precept.

On our return to the camp, Swanepoel informed me that every night during our absence he had been disturbed by a number of Elephants, which approached so near, that they could hear them break the branches of trees, and eat the leaves. I took a turn in the forest, where several young trees were broken, the branches torn, and the young shoots devoured.

This was sufficient information for me, my men had recovered their fatigue, and I thought it more advisable to encounter these animals during the day, than wait their approach by night. We sat out immediately, but had no occasion to go far from our camp, for having ascended a little hill, on the skirts of the wood, I perceived four in a neighbouring thicket. I descended with great precaution, advancing near enough to have a full view of them for half an hour. I observed they were eating the extremities of branches, which before they broke away, they struck three or four times with their trunks, as I imagined, to shake off the insects; after this preliminary, they made a bunch of as many as the trunk would surround, bearing them to the mouth in a direction from left to right, and without much mastication swallowed them. I observed they gave the preference to those branches most covered with leaves, and seemed particularly fond of a tree, whose fruit, when ripe, is yellow, called the *Cerisier* (cherry-tree) in this country.

When I had sufficiently examined them I fired at the head of that nearest me, my shot taking effect, it fell, and in less than ten minutes I was equally successful with the other three. When a troop of Elephants

phants is encountered, if you kill the first you aim at, success is almost sure with the rest; but I shall speak of this singularity hereafter.

We imagined there were more near, but a great noise on one side of us caught our attention, and turning about, one of my Hottentots perceived a young Elephant and shot it. I was very much displeased with him for this, the animal not being bigger than a calf of five or six months old, might easily have been caught and tamed.

Among the four I had shot, was one young male, about seven feet high, his tusks did not weigh more than fifteen pounds each; the highest of the three females was eight feet five inches, the tusks not exceeding the same weight.

A singularity that astonished both myself and people, who assured me they had never

never seen an example of the kind before, and which the sedentary naturalists will no doubt dispute, was, that the Elephant we judged to be the mother of the young male, had but one teat, which was placed in the middle of her breast; this was full of milk, I drew some of it into my hand, it was sweet, but of a disagreeable flavor, and flowed from eight small punctures; the others had two as usual.

The young male which my indiscreet Hottentot had killed, had not yet any tusks, on examination I perceived two small white spots where they would have been, about the size of deer shot. The flesh of this was extremely delicate.

I hoped to have found a fœtus in one of these creatures, but was disappointed; their stomachs were filled with a very transparent liquid, which my people drank of; I tasted it myself, but it occasioned
such

such a disagreeable naufea, that I immediately ran to drink at a spring, about a quarter of a league off.

I had left my men busy in cutting up the Elephants, on my return I thought it very extraordinary, not to find any of them; I could not conceive why they had left their work, and began calling as loud as possible, but was still more astonished at seeing them come out of the Elephants, being employed in securing some interior parts of the creatures, which next to the trunk and feet, are accounted the greatest delicacies.

I had sent one of the Hottentots to my camp, to tell Swanepoel to send me some harnessed oxen and a chain; we had cut off the heads of the Elephants before they arrived, we now fastened them to the chain, but found great difficulty in getting the oxen near enough to draw them; at length

length we accomplished our purpose, and with much labour got them to the camp.

Returning to the thicket, where I had left part of my men, I found it impossible to make my horse pass along, the way being tinged with the blood that flowed from the heads; I was obliged therefore to take him another way, but no sooner did he approach the Elephants, than he started, kicked, and in the end threw me, after which, running a considerable way round, he regained the Camp.

I must now speak of one of those interesting moments, when every impulse of pleasure and transport animates the soul; situations, which the susceptible heart so exquisitely feels, but is so utterly unable to express.

Obliged to return to the Camp on foot,

I perceived a ſtranger on horſeback; it was a Hottentot. Obſerving that he deſigned to come up with me, I ſtopped for him. This proved to be an expreſs from Mr. Boers, who had received orders to enquire after me in all the colonies I had paſſed through, then, following my track, he was to ſeek me in the deſert. This man had exactly fulfilled his commiſſion, having traced the marks of my waggon wheels, which had led him to my different encampments, and at length to myſelf.

Before I quitted the Cape, Mr. Boers had promiſed, that if, during my abſence, any letters arrived from Europe, he would remit them to me, if poſſible; this reſpectable friend had kept his word; in the packet that was now delivered, I found ſeveral from France, which were the firſt I had received ſince my departure.

I cannot describe my impatience on taking this packet from the hands of the messenger; uncertain whether the news was good or ill, I had hardly power to break the seals; it may be easily imagined I did not wait for this 'till I returned to the camp; these letters were from my dearest friend—my wife!—— Impatience prevented my reading — my eyes glanced hastily over them—all were well—were happy!—I was beloved, regretted—friendship reached me though in a desert; overcharging my heart with tender remembrances.——I could neither speak nor sigh; pleasure possessed all my faculties, and deprived me of utterance.

These first transports over, I returned to the camp, where shutting myself up, I gave a free passage to my tears. Having composed my spirits, I immediately prepared to answer these letters, dating mine
from

from *The Camp in Auteniquas, on the day when I killed four Elephants.*

One of thefe letters, which I addreffed to a learned perfon, and which contained feveral interefting details, was fome years ago, handed about Paris, where it was ridiculoufly criticifed. It contained a number of difcoveries, which contradicted the prevailing opinion of that time; thefe I fhall take notice of in my difcription of animals.

In the evening, the camp put in order, our fires made, myfelf feated as ufual, the letters I had been writing on the table, and the Hottentots furrounding me, " Friends," faid I, " this perfon, " your countryman, has been fent by Mr. " Boers, to enquire after my welfare, and " to know if your conduct anfwers his " wifhes; in this," taking up the firft letter that came to hand, " I have inform-
" ed

"ed him, you have hitherto behaved as
"brave and honest men; that during the
"eight months we have travelled toge-
"ther, I have regarded you as the faithful
"companions of my labour; and I have
"entreated him to be under no apprehen-
"sions on your account, as I rely on your
"fidelity with the utmost chearfulness;
"on his return to the Cape, he may in-
"form your friends and relations, that you
"are content and happy."

The proofs of attachment I had received from my friends, their repeated assurances of remembrance and affection, gave me such extreme pleasure, that for the moment I forgot Africa, my collection, birds and hunting, every other consideration being absorbed in the idea of the tenderness, and memory of my friends.

I had this night been rather too generous in the distribution of my tobacco, having

having given them enough to occasion intoxication; this, however, I was now contriving means to prevent; their third pipe drew near the conclusion; after having drank my tea, I ordered a box to be brought and placed before me, which opening, with all the art and myftery of a quack, I drew out that noble and melodious inftrument called a jew's-harp! and beginning to play a lively tune, the pipes of the Hottentots were inftantly laid afide, and every one employed in gazing at me, with mouths half open, arms extended, and fingers ftretched afunder; they might, altogether, have furnifhed an excellent idea to a painter who wifhed to exprefs a group of figures ftruck by the power enchantment. Their aftonifhment was more than equalled by the pleafure they felt; every one, with his head afide, prefenting an attentive ear, that did not lofe a fingle found of my inftrument. I was much diverted; but took the utmoft care not to laugh,

laugh, as that would have spoiled the jest, and lessened the value of my music.

When I ceased playing, I gave the harp to the nearest Hottentot, but had some difficulty in teaching him how to use it, which having accomplished, I sent him to his place; and not wishing to make any difference among them, gave one to each. Some played tolerably, some ill, some horribly; in truth, it was a discord that might have scared a set of furies; even my oxen, frighted at such an unusual noise, bellowed hediously; and in every part of our camp there was a mixture of sounds that exceeded description.

The air of amazement that struck my people on playing this ridiculous instrument, convinced me, that very simple means will astonish untutored minds; and that, probably, the skill of Orpheus, and
harmony

harmony of his lyre, owe all their excellence to the imagination of the poets.

Though they were all in the greateſt
good humour, I was afraid this mirth
might occaſion ſerious conſequences; for
my oxen, who had not yet forgot the
elephants, if too much frighted, might
wander from our camp; by a motion of
my hand I made them underſtand I had
ſomething to ſay; in an inſtant every one
was ſilent.

" My good friends," ſaid I, "I have re-
" galed you with ſome of the beſt tobacco
" you ever taſted, and given every one an
" excellent muſical inſtrument; now let
" us terminate our feaſt by drinking a bum-
" per of brandy each, to the health of our
" abſent friends."

This was a night of revels; *Kees* was
ſeated by my ſide, a place he never failed

to avail himfelf of in the evening; indeed, I had fpoiled him, never eating or drinking any thing but he came in for his fhare; and if I feemed inclined to forget him, he ever took care to remind me, either by munching, or giving me a touch with his paw. He was equally fond of milk and brandy, the latter I ever gave him on a plate, as I had remarked, that in drinking out of a glafs, his greedinefs and precipitation made him draw as much up his noftrils as he took in at his mouth, which occafioned him to cough and fneeze for hours.

Kees, as I have already faid, was feated by my fide, the plate before him, ready for his fhare, while his eyes impatiently followed the brandy bottle, which the Hottentots ferved, with what impatience did he wait his turn! Alas! the unfortunate rogue, that licked his lips in advance, did not know he was going to tafte that bewitching liquor for the laft time; not that
I loft

I lost my friend Kees, though in future I saved his portion of brandy.

I had packed up my dispatches, and was putting on the last cover at the moment the bottle had finished its round, and reached my monkey. I determined for once to cheat him; but without any other intent than to amuse myself with his surprize. The liquor had been just poured into the plate, and he was preparing to seize it, when I added, unseen, a piece of lighted paper; the brandy blazed immediately; Kees screamed and chattered, running away as fast as possible; it was in vain I called and endeavoured to coax him, for being too angry to be easily pacified, he left us and went to his bed. The night was far advanced; and after receiving the thanks of my people, we all retired to rest.

I muſt obſerve, that fear had ſo intirely poſſeſſed poor Kees, that it was in vain I afterwards endeavoured to make him forget what had happened, by offering him his former favourite liquor, which I could never after prevail on him to taſte. Sometimes my men would teaze him, by ſhowing him the brandy bottle, which was ever enough to make him chatter and grind his teeth.

The next day, after having recompenſed the Meſſenger of Mr. Boers, I gave him my diſpatches, and he ſat out for the Cape.

CHAP.

CHAP. XIII.

THE AUTHOR CONTINUES HIS JOURNEY — CROSSES A DANGEROUS MOUNTAIN — MEETS WITH A HOORD OF HOTTENTOTS.

IN the morning I diffected the head of one of the elephants, leaving in the grinders and tufks; during this employment my people returned loaded with the beft parts of the animals, which they cut into long thin flices, that it might dry the more fpeedily when expofed to the fun and wind. Some were employed in breaking the bones, and boiling them for the greafe, which they then put into bladders, and other inteftines. The Hottentot is never negligent in this particular, for befides the confumption on his own perfon, he ufes much in cookery, and indeed we were never overburthened with this article, the greafing of our wheels and traces wafting a large quantity; for without this precaution the leather would foon have been cracked and broken by the heat of the fun. I likewife burned it continually during the night; in default of cotton tearing wicks from my cravats.

This bufinefs took up fome time, and was fcarcely finifhed when one of my men informed us he had feen the print of an elephant's foot at about an hundred paces from the tent; I ran to fee it, and judged the animal to be monftrous, from the largenefs of the impreffion, which was fo frefh, it could not be far off. On

fearching

searching the forest, we soon came near enough for me to shoot him in a vital part, but was surprised he did not fall; I now concluded, that either my gun was not sufficiently loaded, or that the beast was impenetrable. As soon as he felt himself struck, he rushed furiously towards us; but we effectually secured ourselves from his rage, by hastily retiring behind some bushes. After striking the ground for some time, he turned away, and tho' he had lost much blood, went off at so quick a rate, that it would have been impossible to have overtaken him.

I was very much vexed at this escape, it being by much the finest I had ever seen, measuring at least twelve or thirteen feet; and by what we could judge, his tusks might weigh a hundred and twenty pounds each.

Our meat being well dried and packed, we set out on our return to Cayman's-hole, which I had passed on the 13th of April, two months before. The Hottentots I had sent to reconnoitre brought me word, that we might pass the chain of mountains, at a part called *Tete de Diable*, or Devil's Head: We took that road, passing my favorite settlement of *Pampoen Kraal*, of which I took a last farewell.

Having arrived at the foot of the mountain, I ordered the head of the elephant I had dissected, to be put in one of the waggons, and likewise the birds and insects that I had prepared; then leaving my camp once more to the care of part of my faithful attendants, with my waggon, took the road to Mr. Mulder's; for having returned a considerable way, I was no great distance from his dwelling. He was kind enough to promise, that he would remit this collection to Mr. Boers. I now once more

more took leave of Mr. Mulder and his respectable family, and rejoined my people.

Early the next morning we climbed the mountain with great trouble and fatigue; but this was nothing compared to the descension on the other side, which appeared so very difficult, as to alarm and frighten every individual of our company, who stood looking at each other without uttering a word; in fine, we were as men suddenly caught in a trap. To stay on the peak was impossible; we must either descend on one side or the other—thus if we escaped Scylla we fell into Charibdis.

But fortitude and precaution prevail over every obstacle; I recollected that this enterprize was not more difficult for my caravan, than the passage of the Alps had been to innumerable armies; I therefore began to prepare for the dangerous descent

scent, by harnessing only two of my oxen to each waggon, letting only one go down at a time. The first advanced in good order, escorted by all my people; it was necessary to pass over a number of detached points of rock, which formed a kind of steep staircase, that every moment gave the waggon such violent shocks as to threaten to break it to pieces. But this was not the most perilous part of the business; for by means of ropes fastened to the wheels, we sometimes bore them up or let them run, as appeared most convenient; It was when we encountered the smooth, slippery declivities, that we were in the greatest danger. Here the Beasts and carriage were frequently on the very verge of a tremendious precipice. In these situations we got to the highest side of the declivity, and pulled with all our united force the ropes that were fastened to the waggons; for without this precaution, it would have been impossible to

have

have faved either the carriage, or oxen that drew it, from deftruction.

We were obliged to climb this mountain twice, having to fetch our other waggon, which likewife defcended in fafety, after much labour and fatigue.

I confidered this mountain as a barrier nature had placed between me and her choiceft treafures, and I determined, if poffible, to overcome the difficulty; I well knew, that the way from Auteniquas to *Ange-Kloof* was deemed impracticable for any carriage, myfelf being the firft that had made the attempt; this reflection gratified my vanity, efpecially as the enterprize was crowned with fuccefs; but punifhment followed temerity; for I now found myfelf in a moft barren, black defert.

We

We had intirely loft fight of the delightful and fertile country of Auteniquas; the mountains we had croffed, or more properly flid from, intirely obftructing the view of thofe majeftic forefts we had fo long admired. The valley we were now entering appeared a tedious defert, without the leaft appearance of verdure; a fimilar chain of mountains, which extend themfelves in a parallel direction, feeming barely to produce fome miferable plants that grow in fmall clufters, furrounded by the wood, called *Wage-Boom*. The extenfive defert formed between thefe eminences, is of an amazing length, which has given it the name of Ange-Kloof, or Long Valley.

My intention being to go northward, we continued our march for feven hours, croffing the river Queur Boom, which in this valley is no more than a fhallow rivulet, not bearing the leaft appearance of that

that rapid stream, which two months before, had so endangered my life when in pursuit of the Balbuzard.

With some dull melancholy encampments, we continued our wearisome journey; and after twenty-two hours march passed another river, properly called *Krom Rivier* (the Crooked or Winding River) whose current is so amazingly serpentine, that we were perpetually meeting with it, crossing ten times in the course of our journey. As we advanced, the rocks on each side approached nearer to each other; the valley bearing the appearance of a marshy gutter; six leagues of which miserable road tired my oxen exceedingly. We were now come again to Krom-Rivier, for the last time, for it here turns eastward, and falls into the sea, and our steps were directed northward. In this place I left one of my horses that was sick, and unable to travel, not being willing to

stop

stop and wait the event of an uncertain cure. *Ange-Kloof* has some few scattered habitations, that resemble more the dens of animals than the dwellings of men. These people breed but few cattle.

When the east wind blows in this country the cold is extreme; I felt it so during the whole time of my stay in this place; and every morning we had white frosts. I do not know the exact length of this dreary valley; but it took us up forty-six hours to pass it.

After an advance of seven or eight leagues, we crossed the *Diep-Rivier* (the Deep River;) ten leagues from which, on the 7th of August, we encamped on the borders of that called *Gamtoos*, which takes its name from an unfortunate Captain who was shipwrecked there.

We

We had a very steep and dangerous mountain to pass before we reached this spot; two of my oxen were killed in the desert, being embowelled by the pointed rocks; I owed this loss to the carelessness of those who were to conduct the second waggon, but had imprudently left it. The beautiful appearance of this country seemed to promise a recompense for the disagreeable days and severe cold we had encountered, in passing the valley of *Ange-Kloof*.

The first night of my encampment in this place, as I was laying awake in my tent, I thought I heard an uncommon noise; I listened attentively, and found I was not mistaken, plainly distinguishing singing and other expressions of mirth, which seemed at no great distance. I immediately called my men, who had likewise heard it. The question was, whether they were Hottentots or Caffrees; if the latter, they

they were to be feared; not that they thirst for human blood, (as some ignorant writers have advanced) more than other savages, but on account of the odious treatment they have received from the colonists, which leads them to wage perpetual war, supposing vengeance is a natural right.

I shall hereafter relate some facts, that will do more than weak and vain reasoning, in proving which is the greater barbarian, an African savage, or a white colonist.

I was the same colour with their enemies, this was a sufficient reason to be confounded in the number of their victims; I put all my people under arms, we then left our camp, and moved cautiously forward. The noise presently became more distinct, and we discovered some fires; I could not now believe they were Caffrees, as this measure must infallibly have betrayed them, and had they thought to conceal

ceal themselves, they would doubtless have been silent. However, being resolved to guard against the worst that might happen, I placed myself in ambuscade, wishing to surprise them in case they advanced to seize or pillage my camp, at the same time sending two of my people to reconnoitre. These soon returned, informing me it was a false alarm that had disturbed us, it being only a hoord of Hottentots, that were diverting themselves with singing and dancing. I was pleased with this information, as it would afford me an interesting interview on the morrow.

We now returned to the camp, and passed the remainder of the night in great tranquillity. In the morning I was awakened by the warbling of birds, some of which were totally unknown to me. I found part of them very beautiful, the bright copper-coloured Starling, crested cuckow, and the King Fisher, were among the number.

Game appeared to be in great abundance, a multitude of Pheasants rising before me. I likewise saw several Gazells, of that species called *Bos-Bock*, and the facility with which we could take these creatures gave me great pleasure.

While I was amusing myself with shooting birds, I gave my Hottentots permission to visit those who had alarmed us the preceding night. An acquaintance was soon formed, I was introduced, and we were mutually satisfied with each other. The women every night brought us a quantity of milk; these people possessing a large stock of cattle, they gave me some sheep, and a couple of oxen for my waggons; but unwilling to be in their debt, I presented them with knives, steels, and some tobacco.

My men were soon favorites with the Hoord, each obtaining a female companion,

nion, who without ceremony established themselves at our camp for the time we meant to remain here.

I was informed that I might chance to find some Hippopotamuses at the mouth of the river. I had never seen any of these creatures, being therefore only four or five leagues from the sea, and wishing to procure this animal, I proceeded to the spot, but the river was so wide, and the borders so obstructed with large trees, that all my labour was useless.

I passed the days in walking about the environs, and during the night lay in wait, in hopes they would come out of the water to graze, but could never obtain the satisfaction of seeing one. On the other hand, the Elephant and Buffalo were so common and easily killed, that we abounded with provisions, and furnished the former husbands of the ladies, now at our camp, with as much as they pleafed. Being better armed I hunted for them, obliging them by every method in my power, wifhing even in the midft of the defarts of Africa to make myfelf refpected and beloved.

I cannot pafs on without remarking, that though fome hiftorians have given the character of jealoufy to the Hottentots, thefe, at leaft, were not acquainted with that cruel paffion; fhould I in future meet with others poffeffed of it, I fhall declare the fact with equal veracity.

CHAP.

CHAP. XV.

ALARMED BY A TROOP OF ELEPHANTS—REFLECTIONS ON THE DUTCH SETTLEMENTS AT THE CAPE—TAKES LEAVE OF THE HOTTENTOT HOORD—PURSUES HIS JOURNEY.

MY kindness had gained the confidence and good-will of those worthy savages, who entertained so high an opinion of me, that they undertook nothing of moment without first asking my advice.

One day a party of them came to complain that the Hyænas were perpetually thinning their flocks. I readily credited these

these assertions, having recently had one of my oxen devoured by thol. ̤als. Delighted at the thought of hunting with them, I fixed on the next morning for that purpose, and in consequence of this appointment, they were ready at my tent by break of day, to the number of a hundred, well armed with bows and arrows. I immediately put myself at their head, and we began, without loss of time, to beat about the environs with our dogs.

I hoped we should be able to destroy most of the wild beasts that infested this part of the country, but the noise of three discharges of my carbine, (which had brought down as many animals) dispersed and afrighted the rest, driving them to such a distance, that during my stay in this place, no others ever made their appearance.

Some days after an event happened which

which might have been attended with serious consequences. In the middle of the night we were awaked by a horrible din; we soon found it proceeded from a troop of Elephants, which had surrounded our camp. They were so amazingly numerous, that we thought it unadvisable to dispute their passage; my camp, animals and carriages would have been pulverized in a moment; fortunately they made no stay, and we escaped the danger.

At day break we were visited by our neighbours, who had been equally terrified during the night, and came to inform me I must never attack this kind of Elephant, which was very dangerous and malignant, and their flesh good for nothing, being extremely unwholesome; in a word, that these red Elephants——red Elephants! the very name gave me an inclination to see them, and promised me additional information,

mation, for I had never before either heard or read of them.

The animals had retired into the foreft, and gained a fpot only covered with underwood, where it would have been extremely imprudent to attack them. I ordered my Hottentots to take a circle and gain the oppofite fide of the wood, then to fet light to the dried grafs in a number of places, and fire their mufkets, which would oblige the animals to pafs near the foot of a rock upon which I was pofted with fome of my beft markfmen, out of the reach of danger; every thing fucceeded to my wifh. They had no fooner obeyed my orders, than the whole troop took the alarm and approached the fpot where I was ftationed; a dozen difcharges was the reception we beftowed on them, on which they retired with precipitation.

In vain fhould I attempt to defcribe the

the multiplied signs of fury they expressed, on seeing themselves pursued on one side by the blazing bushes and grass, and opposed on the other by our shot, which barred up the only passage by which they could escape the danger. They exerted themselves as much as the enormous weight of their bodies would permit, the loudness of their cries, with the crashing of a number of trees, which they overthrew in their flight, formed altogether a kind of horrid tumult, and struck an awe and terror on my mind, even though I was so sheltered by the rock as to be entirely out of danger.

We wounded one, who had since mingled with the rest in such a manner, that it was impossible to distinguish or get another shot at it, but by its continued bellowing I concluded the hurt was desperate, and that it could not possibly escape. I resolved therefore to seek it the next day

day, and calling my people together we regained the camp.

I was at first surprised at the appearance of these animals, and thought the redness of their skins very extraordinary; but remarking afterwards that the earth in this part of the country was nearly of the same colour, and reflecting that the Elephant passes great part of his time in grovelling in wet marshy places, I concluded it reached no further than the surface, and I was convinced next morning, on finding it dead, that I had not been mistaken in my conjecture.

My people, not intimidated by what our neighbours had reported, of the danger of this provision, cut off the trunk for my use, securing for themselves the other parts of the animal. It was a female, nine feet six inches in height, one of the tusks weighed thirteen pounds, the other ten;

for

for it is observable, that whether male or female, this beast always has the left tusk smaller and more polished than the right, which is occasioned by taking its food from the left side, and their manner of grasping with the trunk the branches on which they feed, preparatory to conveying them to the mouth, occasions a considerable friction on that side, while the right is scarce ever touched; besides this, they are accustomed to turn up the earth with the left tusk.

I began to take great pleasure in this kind of hunting, which I found more diverting than dangerous. I cannot comprehend why travellers have so interlarded their works with tedious accounts respecting the strength and courage of this animal; and so exaggerated the danger to which they are exposed who hunt them. It is true, if a man should be fool-hardy enough to attack an Elephant on an open plain,

plain, if his ball failed to take effect, certain death would be the confequence, as the utmoſt fwiftnefs of his horfe would bear no comparifon with the trot of the furious and powerful enemy in purfuit of him; but if the hunter takes proper advantages, all the ſtrength and fury of the animal muſt yield to his fuperior addrefs. I confefs his firſt appearance impreffes the mind with aſtoniſhment, awe and terror, but one prefently becomes accuſtomed to his afpect.

A prudent man, before he attempts this kind of chafe, will endeavour to difcover the temper, fwiftnefs and recourfes of this animal; but above all, he ſhould fecure himfelf a fafe retreat in cafe of miffing his aim and being purfued; but thefe precautions taken, this hunting is only an amufing exercife, a game in which there is fifty to one for the player.

While

While I stopped in this canton, I was continually varying my encampment, according to my different pursuits, but ever took care to fix my tent on the smiling banks of the *Gamtoos*, where I added considerably to my collection.

The 11th of September, at six o'clock in the morning, we decamped; I had before acquainted our neighbours with my intended removal, who received the news with the most sincere regret; indeed, it was reciprocal; these good people having inspired me with the most cordial attachment. " Is it possible," said I, " that
" so much sweetness and simplicity should
" have been so vilely calumniated!——
" Are these the savages of Africa, who
" have been represented as thirsting for
" the blood of strangers—Who are even
" mentioned with horror?" Their goodness of heart and affibility, had the more effect on me, as I was already plunged in the
bosom

bosom of their deserts, where I saw nothing that could make me dread any dangers for the future.

All this country is inhabited by Hoords of Gomaquais, who differ essentially from the Hottentots of the colonies; indeed, they now seem to have no relation to each other, the former being called savage Hottentots. Before I proceed much farther I shall elucidate this subject, concerning which people in general have formed very imperfect ideas.

They are no longer, as formerly, a nation uniform in its manners, customs and inclinations; the establishment of the Dutch colony was the fatal epocha of their disunion, and of the differences which distinguish them at this day.

When, in 1652, the Surgeon *Riebek*, on his return from India to Amsterdam, opened

opened the eyes of the directors to the importance of a settlement at the Cape of Good-Hope; they wisely thought the enterprize could not be better executed than by the genius that contrived it, and furnished him with full power, and every thing that could contribute to the success of his project.

Arrived in Table-bay, *Riebek*, who was a skilful politician, and happy conciliator, employed every winning art to gain the good-will of the Hottentots; covering with honey the brim of the impoisoned vase. Caught by such deceitful baits, these masters, by prescription, of all this part of Africa, did not fore-see how much the profanation would injure their rights, authorities, repose and happiness. Indolent by nature, true cosmopolites, without inclination to cultivate their land, why should they trouble themselves about strangers settling in a small corner of the country,

country, which was ufelefs, and frequently uninhabited? A little further, or a little nearer, they thought immaterial, provided they found pafture for their flocks, which were the only riches worthy their confideration.

The political avarice of the Dutch entertained great hopes from fuch a peaceable begining; and as they never neglect any advantage that fortune may happen to give them, did not fail to confummate the work, by offering the Hottentots two feducing, and, to them, irrefiftable baits— tobacco and brandy. From this moment, no more liberty! no more pride! no more nature! no longer Hottentots! no longer men! The unhappy favages, bewitched by thefe intoxicating poifons, cannot bear to leave the fource whence they are derived; on the other hand, the Hollanders, who, for a pipe of tobacco, or a glafs of brandy, could purchafe an ox, took care

to

to make every advantage of such profitable neighbours. The colony spreads, increases in strength, and the Hottentots see that power, which dictates laws to all this part of Africa, rise on foundations they cannot now destroy; and triumph over every obstacle that would bar its ambitious cupidity. The fame of its prosperity invites others to settle here, who judging after the common mode, that being most powerful is sufficient authority, commit every act of devastation; cancel every sacred and respectable bond; seizing, in different parcels, all the lands that governors or their favorites find convenient.

The natives thus betrayed, drained, and beset on all sides, take very opposite measures; those who were yet interested in the preservation of their cattle, sought refuge among the mountains, towards the north and north-east, but this was much the smallest number; the others, ruined by brandy

brandy and tobacco, poor, stripped of all could not think of quitting the fatal spot, but regardless of their ancient manners and original (every remembrance of which is now totally extinguished) weakly sold their service to the whites, who, from submissive strangers, became enterprizing imperious masters; whose riches speedily augmented by the multiplied labours of the unfortunate Hottentots, who each day became more degraded, more degenerate.

Some poor miserable Hoords yet exist as they can, in the different cantons belonging to the colonists; these have not even the choice of their own chiefs, who receive this authority from the officers of the company; the governor having an exclusive right to the appointment.

Whenever a chief is nominated, he repairs to Cape-Town, where he receives a large cane, like those of our running footmen,

footmen, with this difference, that the head is only made of copper, on which is engraven, in capital letters, the word *Captain*; from which time the unhappy Hoord (which has long loft its original name) takes that of the new chief, and is called, for example, *The Hoord of Captain Keis*; and Captain Keis becomes the creature, the fpy and flave of adminiftration, and for the Hoord, a new tyrant.

The governor feldom knows the perfon for whom this office is folicited; taking him on the recommendation of one of the colonifts near the Kraal, who obtains the office for one of his creatures, building on his gratitude for the patronage, and expecting to hold all the unhappy vaffals at command, fhould his occafions require their fervice; thus, without preliminaries, without regard to juftice, the defencelefs Hoord is obliged to receive laws from a man who is unequal to the tafk; and the

interest

interest of the multitude is sacrificed to the convenience of an individual.

Such are the people now distinguished by the appellation of, Hottentots of the Cape, or Colonies; but these must not be confounded with the Hottentot savages, called, in derision, *Jackal Hottentots*; who live far from the arbitrary dominion of the Dutch; preserving, in the midst of desarts, their original innocence and purity of manners.

Arrived at a part of my travels, where having intirely left the first-mentioned people behind, I found myself among the second; it is unnecessary to enter into tedious details of the particular differencs that distinguish them; one remark, one certain truth, may suffice: In every part, where the natives live entirely unconnected with the whites, their manners are mild and amiable; on the contrary, an acquaintance with

with the Europeans, alters and corrupts their natural character, which amazingly degenerates; and this remark, which is a melancholy truth, seldom admits of an exception.

When among distant nations, northward of the Cape, under the tropic, I saw whole Hoords surround me with childish curiosity, approaching with confidence, and touching my beard, hair and face; I could not help saying, " I have nothing to fear " from these people; it is the first time " they ever saw an European."

I have given into this digression the more willingly, as I wished to fix some degree of attention on the more serious particulars of my observation ever returning with pleasure to these interesting, though artless details.

The Hoord, who were all very loath to bid adieu, accompanied me to the river *Louri*, four leagues from the Gamtoos; here we stopped to take leave of our good friends, regaling them with some glasses of brandy, and pipes of tobacco. Some of the women, who had attached themselves to my Hottentots, during our acquaintance, wished to follow us; but I had several times remarked, though I feigned not to take notice of it, that disputes had arisen among my men on their account, which were ever attended with neglect of duty, for which reason I peremptorily refused permission for them to accompany us.

One, indeed, had appeared very diligent, taking care of my cows and goats, and washing my linen; these were interested motives for retaining her; but I had another reason that pleaded more powerfully in her behalf.——A mutual and tender

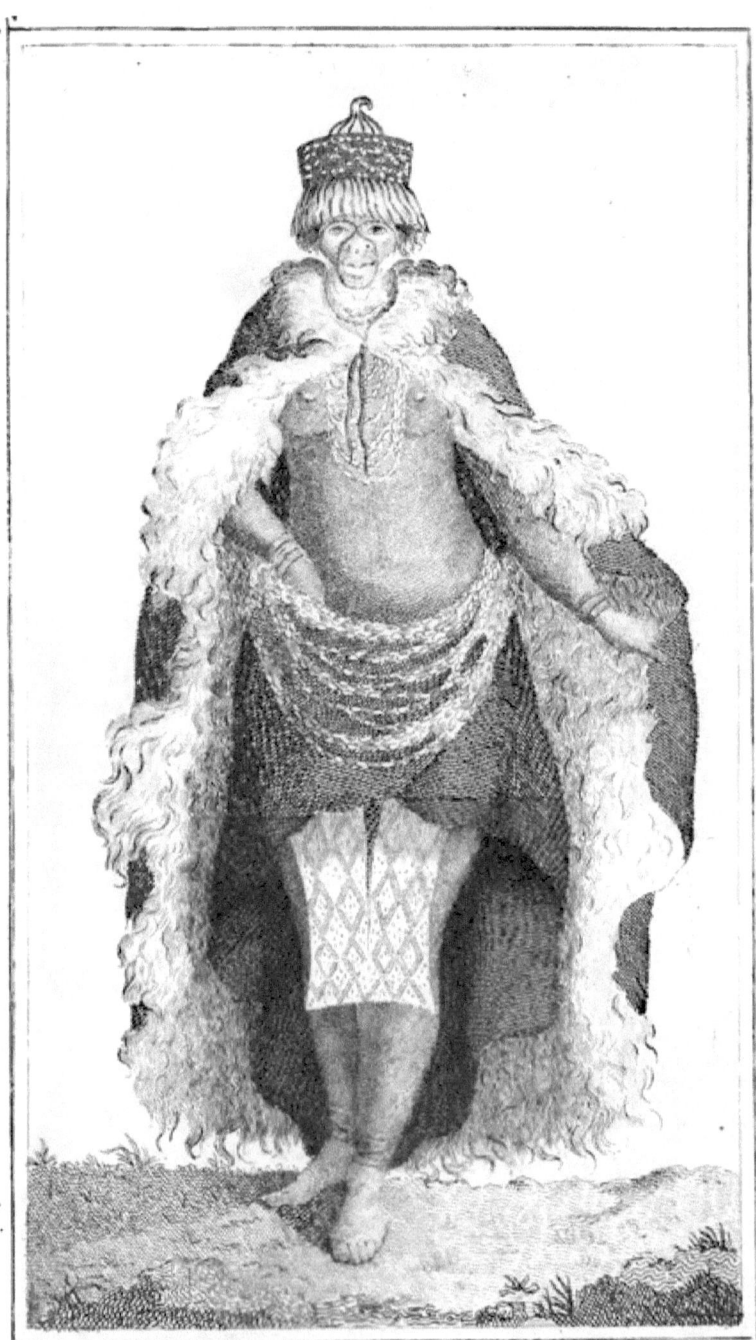

der affection fubfifted between her and my faithful Klaas: Could I rend their hearts afunder, and wound two by one fatal ftroke of unfeeling policy?——Shew myfelf fevere to the man, who, in the hour of danger, would have hazarded his life in my defence?——I care not whether it be called injuftice or weaknefs, I diftinguifhed Klaas from his comrades, enjoying, at leaft, the pleafing idea of having made two beings happy, though it was not in my power to make all fo.

I had no reafon to repent this ftep, for Ragel (the name I gave her) ferved me with the greateft fidelity to the end of thefe Travels.

CHAP.

CHAP. XVI.

JOURNEY CONTINUED—ARRIVES AT A HOTTEN-
TOT KRAAL — DEPARTS ACCOMPANIED BY
THE HOORD—CROSSES THE RIVER SONDAG.

AFTER the departure of the Hoord we continued our way; but a great storm soon obliged us to halt at *Galgebos*; it was five o'clock in the afternoon, and the place so agreeable, that I could willingly have stopped some time, but there was not a single spring near; we therefore continued our rout two leagues further,

water.

How much are we obliged to chance for many interefting difcoveries, which generally fucceed better, becaufe procured by more fimple means, than thofe fuggefted by our imagination, contrivance, or knowledge. — I received a proof of this truth at the place where we now ftopped.

The Hoord I had lately quitted, brought before our departure, a large provifion of milk, a pitcher of which I had placed on my waggon, to drink by the way; but the rain that fell having cooled the air, I found no inconvenience from thirft, and in the evening, going to diftribute it among my men, I found it turned, therefore ordered it to be thrown out for the dogs; but
how

how much was I furprifed to find a quantity of excellent butter, which I owed to the fhaking of my waggon on the road! This difcovery, which I ever after profited by in my travels, furnifhed me likewife with a falutary whey, and contributed, no doubt, towards the good health I conftantly enjoyed.

The fecond day a violent ftorm prevented our departure; it was really tremendous! the hailftones which fell as big as pullets eggs, greatly annoying my cattle. I was obliged to kill one of my goats, who was mortally wounded by them, which was really a lofs to me, fhe being ready to kid.

At length the weather changing, we abandoned the lake; and after crofling two rivers, the little and great *Swaar-Kops*, about the middle of the day, fixed our camp on the banks of the latter.

I foon

I soon after perceived the traces of some animal that was unknown to me; I made my people remark it, who assured me it was the print of a Rhinoceros's foot; while they were fixing my camp, I was following the track; but night aproaching made me lose it, and I returned without success.

Near this second river, which was very large, there was a Hoord of savages, whose kraal consisted of nine or ten huts, containing fifty or sixty people at most.

These Hottentots advised me not to pass the river *Boshies-Man*, that runs near this place, persuading me to turn towards the left, and gain the interior part of the country; as I should, by that means, evade a large troop of Caffrees, who had alarmed the whole canton, spreading destruction where ever they came.

The unhappy inhabitants, to escape a violent death, had abandoned their huts, carrying with them the poor remains of their flocks; in a word, they advised me, if I regarded my safety, not to approach Caffraria. This information had its weight; I assembled my people in order to advise on the best measures, being glad to found their dispositions in this particular. The result accorded with my own intentions; it was, that we should (without going too far out of our way) endeavour to avoid this dangerous troop of Caffrees; and that, as we were already near them, keep guard day and night for fear of a surprize; that we should encamp in future in the open country, and have our oxen watched in their pastures by four men, well armed; my horses were no more to leave the camp, that in case of danger they might be ever ready; my large gun was to remain in the tent, and three fires was the appointed signal for calling

calling those of our people together, whose occupations might have led them from the encampment.

These precautions taken, I mounted my horse, and followed by some of my Hottentots, made a strict search in the environs, to discover if any Caffrees were ranging about, being determined to shoot any that might come with intent to surprise us, if I could not succeed in taking them alive. After dinner we continued our search; the banks of the river were covered with thorny trees; the earth sandy, abounding with underwood, harbouring great quantities of game, some of which I killed for present use.

We saw nothing that could occasion any uneasiness; being therefore, convinced that we were in no immediate danger from these dreaded Caffrees, we raised our camp, and quitted *Swaar-Kops*.

The

The Hoord of Hottentots, alarmed at the very name of thefe dreadful enemies, purpofed to relinquifh their prefent refidence, and eftablifh themfelves at fome diftance from Caffraria; accordingly, when I was ready to depart, they came and entreated permiffion to follow, and put themfelves under the protection of my camp.

Though nothing could poffibly have happened more agreeable to my own wifhes, yet I made a merit of my acquiefence; this kept them in perfect order, while their company encouraged my men, who wanted fuch a ftimulative to fupport their courage.

Befides the advantage of having fuch a reinforcement, my little artillery was equal to whole clouds of affaygays (though the Caffrees are very fkilful in the ufe of them) and would have rendered ufelefs
every

every effort of an army of savages, had I been well supported by my people.

In less than two hours the huts were unfurnished, the effects packed, and placed on the backs of their oxen; I then made half the Hoord set off with the cattle belonging to the Hottentots, two of my men well armed escorting them, having one of my horses, that in case of an attack they might speedily return and inform me. An hour after we followed with the cows, sheep, and all the women and children of the Hoord, mounted on oxen, a part of their men walking behind, escorted by six of my huntsmen.

My waggons proceeded next, guarded by the rest of my men. Mounted on my best horse, I kept galloping around on every side, fearful of some ambuscade; for I was well assured, that in case of a sudden surprise, the whole caravan would have been

been a scene of dismay, and the prey of a moment.

I was armed at all points, a pair of double barrelled pistols in my pockets, a similar pair in my girdle, a double barrelled gun at the pommel of my saddle, a large hanger by my side, and a dagger at my waistcoat button; thus I could have fired ten times in a minute. These weapons somewhat incommoded me, but I resolved not to quit them, as well for my own safety as the confidence with which they seemed to inspire my new auxiliaries, who depending on my power and resolution, continued their way in tranquillity.

This caravan was an amusing, I might say a magnificent spectacle; the circles it was obliged to make in following the different windings of the hills, rocks and interspersed thickets, presented it every minute in a new point of view; sometimes

the

the advanced guard was loft to the fight, then inftantly rifing, I could difcover them far as the eye could reach, flowly climbing the fummit of a mountain, the main body following in good order, the women fuckling or feeding their children, fome crying, others finging or laughing; the men chattering, or fmoaking the focial pipe, regardlefs of their before dreaded enemy.

Not quite fo fatisfied as thefe moving puppets, my eyes were open to every danger; I could not help confidering my critical fituation, at three thoufand leagues from my adopted country, the only one of my colour among fuch a number, nor could I forbear congratulating myfelf on the proof of that confidence which fuffered a ftranger to conduct their fteps through pathlefs defarts, while they implicitly obeyed and relied on him as the fole author of their prefervation.

We had not travelled far, before our dogs, who were beating about the thicket, made a sudden stand, and began barking; fear immediately seized the whole company, whose imaginations formed an ambuscade of Caffrees; for my own part, I could not give into this absurd opinion, as my advanced guard (who were in sight though at a great distance) had passed in perfect safety, and were continuing their rout in good order. On examination into the cause of the alarm, I found my dogs had surrounded a Porcupine, which was defending itself in the midst of them; I shot it on the spot, and lest the Hottentots should be alarmed at the report of my piece, returned immediately and endeavoured to laugh them out of the panic this little adventure had occasioned.

The porcupine defends itself with great resolution, its quills shielding it from an attack; its common manner of repulsing

a

a dog is, by throwing himself sideways on the foremoft, who thus touched, returns no more to the charge, as fome of the quills are fure to remain in his flefh, which generally difcourages even the moft ferocious. One of my Hottentots was ill for more than fix months by a wound he received in the leg from one of thefe animals.

Mr. Mallard, an officer in the regiment of Pondicherry (when at the Cape) having one day teafed a Porcupine, the enraged creature wounded him in the leg, which almoft occafioned his lofing the limb, and notwithftanding every poffible care, he fuffered cruelly for four months, one of which he paffed in bed.

The Porcupine is excellent eating, and frequently ferved at the politeft tables at the Cape.

After an hour and a half's march we halted,

halted, but stopped no longer than was sufficient to gather a good quantity of salt from the banks of a salt-water lake, which was in our way, two leagues from which I rode a little to the left, in order to view the remains of some habitations that had been plundered and afterwards burnt by the Caffrees; nothing remained but pieces of the walls, blackened and calcined by the flames, which presented a horrible image in the desart.

An hour after we reached our advanced guard, which had stopped on the borders of the *Kouga,* where we pitched our camp.

The *Kouga* (properly speaking) is nothing more than a rivulet, whose water runs very slowly, some only now remained in hollows, where we found a great number of excellent Tortoises, but very small, the largest not weighing more than three pounds. Before night I caused a
kind

kind of inclosure to be made, of bushes and arms of trees, for our cattle. While the men were thus employed, the women were picking up all the dry wood they could find, to light up several fires; this was indispensibly necessary, to prevent being surprized by the Caffrees, or an attack from Lions, who are very numerous in this Canton.

We remained here 'till the twentieth, when, (just as our provisions were expended) I was fortunate enough to kill three Buffaloes and two Bubales. On the borders of the rivulet I likewise procured some Pintadoes, or speckled fowl, exactly resembling those of Europe; when well boiled they were tolerably good, but roasted or broiled worth nothing; these indeed appeared to be very old. I also found some other species of birds, and among others the *Barbus*.

We continued our journey in the same order we had before obferved, and had not proceded above an hour, when our advanced guard halted, and fent me word, that they had difcovered the track of human feet. The fears of our people immediately formed a large body of Caffrees, who were now heard in every wind. I haftened to the fpot, and examined thofe marks; they did not appear quite frefh, yet it was a ferious difcovery, and I felt it was not to be neglected, nor any time loft in putting ourfelves in a pofture of defence, for which purpofe we folded the cattle and arranged our camp in the beft manner poffible.

This bufinefs compleated, I fet forward attended by my two beft markfmen, and followed the track for more than an hour, which conducted us to a place where we found the remains of a fire unextinguifhed, and fome bones of a fheep perfectly frefh, by by all which it was evident that savages had paſſed the night there. On fight of the bones I could not be perſuaded they were Caffrees, as thoſe people never breed any ſheep, though it might be poſſible they had pillaged ſome from their enemies. Uncertain what to believe, I continued my ſearch, 'till at length, weary of beating about the country, and finding the track carried us too far, we returned to our camp. The night paſſed in great tranquillity; the day following was uſhered in by a violent ſtorm, and continued rain, which obliged us to keep cloſe in our tents. On the morrow we continued our rout, and were under the diſagreeable neceſſity of croſſing the *Kouga* fourteen times, which from its various windings we encountered every quarter of an hour. This river runs on a bed of ſtones and rock, which ſhook our waggons very much, and obliged us by the fatigue it occaſioned to halt rather early.

We passed the night by the *Drooge-River* (Dry-River.) Being now so large a company, it took a considerable time of an evening to fix our camp, tend the cattle, gather wood for fires, and cook the victuals, which altogether was a laborious, though an indispensible duty. Our dogs at this place were our purveyors, the country abounding with Pintadoes, who about sun set roost by hundreds on the surrounding trees, making a perpetual and disagreeable noise, that alarmed our dogs, and occasioned them to bark violently at the birds, who being apprehensive of danger sought security at a greater distance from these disturbers; but the wings of this fowl being small, the weight of their bodies soon brought them to the ground, where they became an easy prey, furnishing us with plenty of food without the expence of a single charge of powder.

We afterwards endeavoured to procure another

another recruit by the fame means, but the remaining Pintadoes (poſſibly grown wiſe from the misfortunes of their late companions) would not now quit the trees, but a few ſhot procured us as many as we pleaſed. During the night we conſtantly heard the roaring of Lions at a diſtance.

On the twenty-third, after ſix hours march, we arrived at a fine river, called *Sondag*, which was at this time at its greateſt height; the ſky alſo lowering and bearing every appearance of rain, made us apprehenſive of being ſtopped by an overflow, we therefore prepared ſome rafts, and cutting a ſufficient quantity of wood and materials to encloſe our beaſts on the oppoſite ſhore, we embarked our waggons by parcels, with all our effects, and half the people; theſe encamped, on their landing, under the conduct of Swanepoel; the beaſts, as on a former occaſion, ſwam over. The day following I joined them with the reft; thefe preparations and the re-eftablifhment of our waggons, &c. occupied us to the end of the month.

In this interval I procured a number of birds, and' falted feveral Coudous, but had nearly loft my poor Kees; an account of which incident may give an idea of my fimple and uniform method of living. I was juft fitting down to dinner when I heard the warbing of a bird that I was unacquainted with, my meal was forgot in an inftnt, I fnatched up my gun, left the tent, and in a quarter of an hour returned wh the bird but was much furprifed to find my table empty. Kees having difpatched my provifion with wonderful celerity.

I had punifhed him very feverely the night before for ftealing my fupper, therefore could not have fuppofed he would have

have so soon forgot it; Kees however disappeared; this was by no means unusual to him in similar cases, though he used constantly to return about tea time, with an air of innocence, unconcernedly occupying his usual place by my side, but this evening he was missing, and the next day we saw nothing of him.

I now felt some uneasiness, fearing he was entirely lost. On the third day one of my men who had been fetching water, saw my monkey ranging in the neighbouring trees, but the rogue, at sight of him, ran away and concealed himself.

I immediately went in search of him, beating all the environs with my dogs, suddenly I heard a scream similar to that of Kees, when I used to return from shooting and had left him behind. I immediately stopped, and soon perceived him in a tree, half concealed by a large branch;

I enticed him by every means I could think of, but in vain; he would not trust to these signs of friendship, but obliged me to climb the tree, when he immediately suffered himself to be taken.

Pleasure and fear alternately marked his actions; I returned with him to the camp, it was there he expected his punishment; I had a great mind to tie him up, but that would have deprived me of the amusement his tricks afforded, I therefore pardoned him; perhaps he had before been punished when he did not deserve it, for his character of thievery made me ready enough to believe what was said to his disadvantage; possibly I might be wrong in this, as it was far from unlikely that my Hottentots had sometimes committed what poor Kees bore the blame of.

CHAP.

CHAP. XVII.

THE AUTHOR CONTINUES HIS JOURNEY — ARRIVES AT SEVERAL DESERTED HABITATIONS — AN ALARM — IS JOINED BY SOME FRESH HOTTENTOTS — DISAGREEMENT AND PARTING.

THE *Sondag* is a river whose source is in high mountains, that are always covered with snow, which has procured them the name of *Sneuw Bergen*, (Snow Mountains.) This river is encreased by several small streams, and discharges itself into the sea at about ten leagues from the spot where I then was.

The

The first of October we continued our journey, and in seven hours came to the ruins of a pillaged habitation, which we soon after passed. At four we took our station by the side of a lake, and were very happy in having large fires, as several Hyænas and two Lions were this night particularly troublesome, which obliged us to watch and fire at them very often, this being the only means of keeping them at a distance, so determined did they appear in their resolution to visit us.

At day break we saw a great number of *Spring-Bock*, I therefore determined to hunt the whole day, our provision being nearly exhausted. The conducting a whole Hoord, together with their cattle, is a talk that requires some little care and foresight, for without it, in these deserts, the whole body would frequently be in danger of perishing for want of food; this, however, was not likely to be the case, as we were

fortunate

fortunate enough to kill seven of the Gazells.

These animals are very swift, but easily overtaken by a person on horseback, as they assemble in flocks like sheep, and crowd together in such a manner as mutually to obstruct each others speed, and a ball well directed, will sometimes pass through two or three of them.

The day following we moved sooner than we intended, on account of the badness of the water; in four hours we procured better, by meeting with a branch of the *Sondag*.

Our oxen now began to be so fatigued from the extreme heat, that we were fearful of losing some of them on the way, though we gave them as much relief as possible by frequently shifting their burthens.

On

On the fourth we quitted the stream entirely, and travelled but three leagues, the heat being insupportable, and the cattle not recovered from the fatigue of the preceding day.

On the fifth we sat forward at three in the morning; at seven reached another abandoned habitation, the proprietors of which (actuated no doubt by fear) had not removed any part of their effects, every utensil being in its proper place. As there was not the least mark of fire or any other devastation, it plainly proved their sudden flight was caused by a false alarm. The heat being still excessive, we took up our quarters here, but I would not permit my people to touch the most minute article; after resting a while we departed, and continued our march for four hours.

On the morrow we passed two habitations deserted like the former, and in the same

same state. We continued our way, and four hours march brought us to the banks of the little river Vogel, where we just stopped to bait, as our oxen wanted water and food. At twelve the sky became overcast, and thick clouds obscured the face of the sun; I profited by this circumstance, hoping to gain *Agter-Bruyntjes-Hoogte*, but meeting with a lake at the foot of the mountain, it engaged us to stop and encamp.

During the night our fires were perceived by some Hottentot savages; as these people approached they were discovered by our dogs, who gave us notice of it by barking violently, and running backwards and forwards in great agitation. The major part of my people were persuaded they were Caffrees; and fear, as on a former occasion, presented, on every side, the dreaded enemy, from whom they wished to fly, and trail to the bushes for safety, ty, rather than unite in a well-armed determined body, resolutely bent to defend their lives and property from a lawless and daring assailant.

Klaas and myself were greatly exasperated at their cowardice, even the venerable Swanepoel joined in trying to inspire these pusillanimous Hottentots with courage; protesting, that whatever might be the event, he would hazard even life itself in my service. In the midst of our confusion, a voice was heard, which, in tolerable dutch, entreated we would call off our dogs; this we instantly did, and immediately discovered the authors of this dreadful alarm, to be a small body of peaceful Hottentots. I desired them to approach; the men were about fifteen in number, besides women and children, and were now travelling to avoid the fury of war; they told me, that when I had passed the mountains, I should find several

veral habitations deserted, whose late possessors had assembled together to repel
the enemy; but that, for their own part,
they resolved totally to quit this district,
and draw nearer the Dutch colonies, as
the Caffrees were raging about the country,
vowing destruction to all that fell in their
way.

Having passed the night in conferences
of this nature, and learnt all I was de-
sirous of knowing, their information did
not dispose me to consider the Caffrees as
ferocious animals, nurtured with human
gore, sparing neither age nor sex, and totally regardless of the rights of hospitality.
I was sufficiently acquainted with the disposition of the Colonists to place to their
account the calumnies with which the
unfortunate Caffrees have been loaded.

They are not naturally cruel, living like
the other natives of this part of Africa,
on the simple produce of their flocks;

their nourishment milk, and skins their cloathing; peaceful by nature, warriors only from necessity; and by no means a nation whose name ought to inspire horror.

As I wished to be informed of the real motives of these cruel wars, the Hottentots, on being particularly questioned, told me without reserve, that the perpetual vexations and cruel tyranny of the Colonists, was the sole cause; they likewise informed me, that the Boshis-Men (a set of vagabond deserters, of no particular nation, living by rapine, and robbing alike Caffree, Hottentot or Colonist) would willingly instigate the Caffrees to distress, and put in one general proscription, both Colonist and Hottentot; considering the latter as spies, attached to the whites, and employed to ensnare them with the greater facility; perhaps this idea is not totally without foundation, but cannot, by any means, extend to the distant Hoords. Thus

the

the innocent suffer with the guilty; for how should savages make a distinction that civilized people are frequently incapable of? Amongst other information I learned, that the Caffrees had procured a few fire-arms from some of the pillaged habitations, or from the Hottentot Colonists who had been set on unawares.

These people likewise gave me a long detail of the attacks and combats they had sustained, in which the Caffrees had ever been worsted; this did not seem at all surprizing, as the assaygay, which is their most destructive weapon, and which they throw with exquisite skill, is by no means comparable to fire-arms, especially when directed by marksmen who seldom or ever miss their aim.

I found myself particularly interested in what I heard, and felt an ardent desire to serve these unfortunate beings; their unhappy fate so much excited my compassion, that could I but have perfuaded my people to accompany me, I would gladly have traverfed fifty leagues of Caffraria, and run all hazards, to attempt the eftablifhment of a lafting peace; but on difclofing my wifhes, no one feconded my intention; and all perfuafion was ufelefs to this terror-ftruck people, for which reafon I was rather fparing of my reproaches, tho' I was far from being fo to the Colonifts, whofe affiftance I requefted two days after.

A misfortune which had lately happened, contributed not a little to heat my imagination. I was informed, that fix weeks before, an Englifh fhip, the Grofvenor, Eaft-Indiaman, had been wrecked on the coaft, that part of the crew and paffengers, efcaping the turbulent element, unfortunately fell into the hands of the Caffrees, by whom they were barbaroufly deftroyed, the women excepted who were referved to undergo ftill greater hardfhips; fome few, it was fuppofed, posed, had escaped, and were now wandering on the coast, or exploring melancholy and almost impenetrable forests, where they could not fail in the end of perishing miserably. Amongst these unfortunate people, were several French officers, prisoners of war, who were coming to Europe.

My heart was wounded by this afflicting detail; a thousand projects bewildered my head. I could not be above fifty leagues from the unfortunate spot—— Various means occurred to succour the unhappy sufferers, whose situation was so truly deplorable. I proposed these means to my companions, but every proposal was refused. In vain I offered presents, prayers, intreaties, nay, even threatenings had no more weight; to these last I must infallibly have fallen a sacrifice, had I not been seconded by three of my bravest fellows, and also shewn the utmost resolution, both in words and actions, being obliged to clap a pistol to the head of one of the

most

moſt refractory; however, nothing I could do was of any ſervice to my favourite project; the Hoord I had given leave to accompany us, told me they were *free*, nor did they conſider me as their chief, and that they would immediately depart with the fifteen Hottentots recently arrived; even my own men declared they would not hazard being cut to pieces by the Caffrees, and ſeconded the general cry, openly avowing their determination to return to the colonies, if I ſtill perſiſted in my reſolution.

The repreſentations and perſuaſions of Klaas and myſelf at length brought over two, who conſented to hazard themſelves with me; Swanepoel was one, but four was inſufficient. In vain I painted to theſe ſavage Hoords, the ingratitude with which they repaid the ſervices I had rendered them; in vain I called them weak cowards, and worſe than Caffrees; all did but encreaſe their fears, and inſpire them
with

with hatred to myfelf. Difmay was legibly written on their countenances; I therefore was filent, ordering a ftrict guard to be kept, as the night was far advanced; I then retired to my tent.

At day break I was informed that the ftrangers were moving, with their wives, children and cattle. I ordered no notice to be taken of this, and without lofs of time prepared likewife to depart.

In four hours we traverfed the mountain of Agter-Bruyntjes-Hoogte, where we had a refrefhing fhower; after which we travelled four hours more, and then encamped for the night.

In our way we faw many uninhabited tenements, which perhaps belonged to thofe we had juft parted from. The foil in this part of the country appeared in general to be good; the mountains covered with lofty trees, and the plains with the

mimofa

mimofa-nilotica, and abound with Gazells and *Gnous*; the latter, though good eating, are inferior to the Gazells. By what I had learned from the fifteen Hottentots, I judged I could not be far from the spot where the Colonifts meant to affemble; and I flattered myfelf I fhould find among them fome, whofe hearts would readily enter into my pacific meafures with the Caffrees, and affift in every endeavour to fuccour the unhappy people that had been fhipwrecked; the image of whofe misfortunes perpetually followed me.

How cruel a fituation for women! condemned to drag a painful life in all the horrors of agonizing defpair. A defire to procure them liberty, to bring them away with me, employed all my thoughts, and deafened me to every obftacle, making me impatient to join the affembled Colonifts.

The Tranflator conceives that it cannot fail to be acceptable to the public to learn, that

that Mr. Carter, the Painter, has been prevailed on to publish a most interesting Narrative of the whole of this unfortunate event, which he had an opportunity of writing from the testimony of one of the poor fellows who survived, and with whom he sailed back again to India; and he is now actually engaged in making drawings for engravings to accompany that work, which will appear as soon as they can be well executed.

CHAP. XVIII.

THE AUTHOR ARRIVES AT BRUYNTJES-HOOGTE —QUITS IT WITH DISGUST—AUGMENTS HIS TRAIN—CONTINUES HIS JOURNEY.

WE began our march at day-break, and in three hours discovered the wished-for settlement; the inhabitants of which

which perceived me at a diftance; and I could fee them affembling, and frequently turning to gaze at me with an air of alarm, occafioned, no doubt, by the fight of my baggage and attendants. I fpurred my horfe, and foon joined them, fpeaking with great politenefs, at the fame time makeing known my name, and pretending I travelled by authority of the Dutch government, to whom I muft give an account of my difcoveries; the conclufion of this difcourfe feemed to have great weight with them, and I was received with every demonftration of joy.

They owned that my beard had puzgled them, which was now of eleven months growth; nor could they tell what to make of my weapons, my carriages, and large retinue. They had frequently heard of me, and of the numerous inconveniences I had fuftained; but had lately been informed, I had failed in a veffel that lay

at

at anchor in the bay of Blettenberg, bound for the Isle of Bourbon; they therefore did not entertain the most distant idea of seeing me. I was then obliged to bear with being asked a hundred questions without having time allowed to answer one.

Before I declared the motives that brought me here, and my resolution to penetrate into Caffraria, I expressed my astonishment that none of them had already attempted to relieve those unhappy Europeans, whose miserable situation they were not unacquainted with; and that I now hoped to find some, whose hearts would prompt them to go with me towards the coast where the vessel was cast away; as the Dutch government, I made no doubt, would amply reward those who undertook so glorious an enterprize; I likewise added, that as the vessel was not yet gone to pieces, they might possibly find

find effects enough in the wreck to enable them to pafs their lives comfortably. This laft motive feemed to have its weight; and I hoped a happy iffue from the following anfwer: "That if things were as I had faid, it was right to affift thefe unhappy people, who were in truth their fellow creatures and brethren."

One of the moft cunning poltrons of the fet, whom avarice alone interefted, added, "That the Caffrees had probably ftripped the veffel of all that was worth looking after, and in that cafe, the rifk they run in leaving their wives and children to the mercy of the favages, could not by any means be counterbalanced by a precarious profpect of amending their circumftances."

'Tis true, there was not much to tempt them to undertake the journey, as they could have no view of purloining cattle from

from their enemies, having divided twenty thousand since the commencement of hostilities; the few that remained were secured, by the Caffrees having drove them into places of perfect security.

I used my utmost endeavours to combat the reasons of this man, but in vain; his avaritious arguments confuting all that humanity could urge; and as they could not be assured of gain, they absolutely refused their assistance.

It was a vain attempt to alter such hardened obstinacy; I could not, however, restrain my rage, which broke out into threatenings of the displeasure they would incur from the Dutch government; concluding with wishing them surrounded by thousands of Caffrees, and lest their conduct should influence some of my people, I abruptly broke off the discourse, and continued my journey.

I ob-

I observed that these Colonists had among them numbers of a mixed race, between a white and a Hottentot; they are generally courageous and enterprizing, adhering more to the Colonist than to the Hottentots, whom they regard as their inferiors; they are always the first to march against the Caffrees, signalizing themselves in every rencontre; a knowledge of this made me resolve to leave three of my men, in whom I could confide, in order to confort with, and if possible engage some of them to follow me, particularly those who knew the country and language of the Caffrees. I instructed them sufficiently in regard to their conduct, and appointed the river *Klein-Vis*, where I was then going, for our place of rendezvous, which we reached and crossed after three hours travel through very bad roads. We rested here for the night, as I could not possibly expect to hear the event of my people's negociation until the next day.

In this place I perceived some marks that denoted the lion to be no stranger here; therefore took the necessary precautions to prevent a surprize, both from that animal, and likewise from the Caffrees. I should have felt but little uneasiness on account of the latter, had it been possible to inform them that I was neither of the *nation* nor of the *disposition* of their persecutors; but they might fall on my camp unawares, and do me great damage before I could come to an explanation; this consideration, therefore, engaged me (contrary to my usual custom) to choose an elevated encampment, from which I could see to a considerable distance all round.

Here I fixed my tent, placing the waggons and cattle near us. At the distance of a few paces I constructed some false huts, fixing my fire-arms within gun shot of them, and covering our retreat with branches

ches of trees, so that it could not be perceived; here we determined to pass the night; that in case an enemy presented, and attempted to surprise our camp, we might have a manifest advantage.

The night was by no means quiet, the barking of our dogs giving us a great deal of inquietude, and rendering it impossible to sleep. At day break I discerned at some distance my expected Hottentots, they brought with them three strangers, one of whom, named *Hans* (the son of a white man and Hottentot woman) had lived a good while among the Caffrees, and spoke their language with great facility. Some glasses of Brandy soon gained me his confidence, and procured me information of the present state of affairs.

What I learned from this man confirmed me in the opinion I had before formed, that the Caffrees are in general harmless

harmless and peaceable, but being continually pillaged, harrassed, nay often murdered by the whites, they are obliged to take up arms in their own defence. He likewise informed me, that the report of this Nation being barbarous and bloody, was industriously circulated by the Colonists, in order to justify the attrocious thefts they were daily guilty of towards them, and which they wished to have pass for reprisals. That they often formed pretences of losing cattle, purposely to make inroads into the Caffree settlements, exterminating whole Hoords without distinction of age or sex, carrying away their herds, and laying waste the country; this means of procuring cattle appearing much easier than the slow method of breeding them, and in this manner *Hans* assured me, twenty thousand had been obtained the last year, at which time he was an eye witness of the following instance of inhumanity.

In destroying a small settlement of Caffrees, a child about twelve years old escaped the general carnage, by concealing himself in a hole, but unfortunately was discovered by one of the marauders, who determined to make a slave of his prize; the commander of this barbarous detachment peremptorily laid claim to the poor little prisoner; the Colonist as firmly refused to deliver him up, which so enraged the savage leader, that he ran with the utmost fury at the innocent object of the dispute, exclaiming—"If I must not have him, neither shalt thou," and accompanied these words with lodging the contents of his piece in the breast of the unfortunate victim, who instantly died.

In addition to the above, I was likewise told that these ferocious extirpators would sometimes amuse themselves with placing their prisoners at a stated distance, in order to try their superiority over each other as expert

expert markſmen. Were I ſo diſpoſed, I need not ſtop here, but particular conſiderations and powerful motives cloſing my lips, I can only ſhudder and be ſilent. I have ſaid enough to ſhew what thoſe Coloniſts are, whom Government leave to their exceſſes, becauſe they are either too weak, or too puſillanimous to ſtrike at the root of this dreadful enormity. Thus then are committed all the horrors that imagination can form an idea of, by people ſubject to a republican ſtate, diſtinguiſhed from all others, for its ſimplicity of manners, and truly philanthropic ſpirit.

If at any time the Governor receives advice of theſe atrocious deeds, the diſtance, (and other reaſons which perhaps are not prudent to enquire into) bring them to town ſo ſoftened and disfigured, that they are ſcarcely taken any notice of.

A Coloniſt who lives two hundred leagues

gues up the country, arrives at the Cape, to complain that the Caffrees have taken all his cattle, and intreats a *Commando*, which is a permission to go, with the help of his neighbours, and re-take his property; the Governor, who either does not, or feigns not to understand the trick, adheres strictly to the facts expressed in the petition; a preamble of regular information would occasion long delays—a permission is easily given—'tis but a word—the fatal word is written, which proves a sentence of death to a thousand poor savages, who have no such defence or resources as their persecutors.

Thus the monster (regardless of religion) having compleated his business at the Cape, returns with an inhuman joy to his villainous accomplices, and extends his *Commando* as far as his interest requires; the massacres this occasions, is but the signal for other butcheries; for

should

should the Caffrees have the audacity to attempt regaining any part of their lost herds, the confusion recommences, and only ceases when there are no more victims or no more plunder.

This perpetual war, or rather robbery, continued during the whole time of my stay in Africa. It was not the speculations of commerce, or love for any particular service that directed my steps, but my natural inclination, and a fondness of new discoveries. I am more acquainted with the interior parts of the country, than with the Colonies of the Cape, or the Cape itself; no personal interest therefore can make me suspected of partiality. I have observed that the political eye is open too late to the establishments that daily spread to such a distance from the seat of Government; the mere name of authority is too insufficient to check the disorders that multiply and vex the interior part of the country; this being the cafe, fhould it ever happen that the Caffrees, and the neighbouring nations, (who have alfo caufe of complaint) were to unite, their junction, at leaft, would bode no good to the Colonifts, nay poffibly might in time affect the Cape itfelf.

At prefent, the government have more than one means to prevent thefe misfortunes; but it is certainly time to employ thofe means, as dangers ever encreafe by delay. I have before obferved, that the bare iffuing a precept is of no effect; this the following inftance will plainly verify: A governor being informed of fome cruel vexations practifed againft the favages, fummoned the author to the Cape, to render an account of his conduct; the culprit did not even deign to anfwer the order, but continued harraffing and pillaging in his ufual manner, and his difobedience was overlooked and forgotten.

One day I was speaking of these abuses to some Colonists, who told me, that several of them had received similar mandates from the governor, to which they paid no attention. I answered, I was amazed then that the governor did not accompany his orders with a detachment, and in case of refusal, conduct the culprit under a good escort to town. "Do you know," said one of them, "what would " be the result of such an attempt? We " should instantly assemble, and kill half " the soldiers, whom we would salt and " send back by those we had spared, with " promises to do as much for others that " came on the same errand."

Men of this temper are not easily managed; nor is it impossible, but these turbulent spirits may one day throw off the yoke intirely, and give laws to their present nominal rulers; nor would this prove by any means a work of difficulty, especially

ally, if some informed, artful individual, was to gain the good-will and confidence of the multitude, who already know too well the facility of the enterprize, and advantages of success. He need only represent, in lively colours, that they could raise upwards of ten thousand skilful markfmen, whose every shot would carry death; and with very little hazard or danger, might overthrow any force government could send into these parts: That riches and abundance would pour in upon them the moment they threw off the oppressive, and frequently tyranic, power of their rulers, whose regulations are in direct opposition to every species of private advantage: That inhabiting a favorable climate, possessors of a fine country, furnished with plenty of game, they might exchange the products of their lands and flocks for every article of luxury, which foreign countries would be glad to bring to the numerous ports and roads with which

which their coast is furnished; while population increasing with riches, they might enjoy all the advantages of an extensive commerce.

These reflections are not new at the Cape, and are, perhaps, the best excuse for their apparent remissness in punishing the enormous outrages of the Colonists; well knowing the turbulent disposition of these people, naturally robust, and bred in their native woods.

Another motive, which at the time I was in that country might possibly make them slacken the reins of authority, was the assistance they hoped for from these people, if the English had attacked Cape-Town, as was expected, in the year 1781. And the following trait may shew they are to be depended on.

On a falſe alarm being ſpread, in leſs than four and twenty hours near twelve hundred of them arrived, and offered their aſſiſtance; and would immediately have been followed by others, had they not received orders to the contrary.

I ſhould lead my readers into an error, if what I have ſaid induced them to imagine, that theſe Coloniſts are ſo many Cæſars; this is by no means the caſe, nor would that account agree with the details already given of their wars with the Caffrees.

Born among the rocks and foreſts, a hardy, or rather ſavage education, renders them amazingly robuſt and ſtrong; accuſtomed from their early youth to lay wait for the dangerous animals of Africa, they are expert at a ſurpriſe, or ambuſcade; but I much queſtion whether they would dare to face an enemy in the open field, or

if

if routed ever return to the charge; being unacquainted with that innate magnanimity which infpires true courage.

From a recollection of the adventure of Saldanha-Bay, it may eafily be judged whether I have exaggerated in this account of their character.

It is not thus with the women, the principal part of whom have real prefence of mind and courage, fearing no obftacles, and calmly facing danger; managing a horfe, and firing a mufket with as much fkill as their hufbands; are more indefatigable, never flying from an enemy and may be truly ftiled amazons.

I knew a widow that managed her own plantation, who, when the wild beafts attacked her flocks, mounted on horfeback and purfued them with the greateft intrepidity: never quitting the chafe 'till fhe she either killed, or drove them from the canton.

In one of my journies, two years after, in the country of the Namaquias, I saw, in a lonely habitation, a young woman of about twenty, who always accompanied her father on horseback, when at the head of his people he attacked the Boshis-men, who often gave them disturbance; following these wretches, regardless of their impoisoned arrows, with the utmost spirit and bravery; overtaking them in their flight, and shooting them without pity. The annals of the Cape make mention of a great number of women, who have distinguished themselves by actions of bravery, that might do honor to the most courageous of our sex.

On my return to the Cape, the common topic of discourse was the tragical adventure of a widow, who had lived at a distant solitary

solitary habitation with her two sons, the eldest of them about nineteen. One gloomy night the family was awakened by the lowing of the cattle, in an inclosure, at a small distance from the house; they immediately seized their weapons, and running to the spot, found a lion had broken through the fence, and was making terrible havock among the oxen. It was only necessary to enter the inclosure, fire and kill the animal, who had no chance of escape; but neither her sons, slaves, or Hottentots, had sufficient courage to attempt it; this undaunted woman, therefore, entered alone, and armed with a musket, approached the scene of confusion; the obscurity of the night prevented her seeing the furious beast 'till she was close by him; she immediately fired her musket, but was so unfortunate as only to wound the animal, who rushed on her in an instant.

The screams of the unfortunate mother brought the sons to her assistance.—Furious—desperate—distracted—they fell on the tremendous animal and killed him (though too late) on the mangled body of their parent.

Exclusive of the deep wounds she had received in the throat, and different parts of the body, the lion had bit off one of her hands at the wrist.——Assistance was ineffectual; she died the same night, amidst the vain lamentations and regret of her children and servants.

CHAP.

CHAP. XIX.

THE AUTHOR SENDS MESSENGERS TO KING PHAROO — ARRIVES AT KOKS-KRAAL — ENDEAVOURS TO SECURE IT FROM ANY SUDDEN ATTACK.

HANS gave me every explanation in his power relative to Caffraria, informing me that the spot we were now upon was formerly part of the dominion of a puissant Chief, who now resided thirty leagues from us, towards the North, and was called King Pharoo. He likewise persuaded me to go forward, maintaining that so far from having any danger to apprehend from the inhabitants, they would be well pleafed to fee me, in hopes that on my return to the Cape, the defcription I fhould give of their manners, difpofitions and way of life, would fo far efface the ill impreffions the Colonifts had given of them, that they might obtain peace and tranquillity, the only favor they afked of the whites.

This reafoning, on the firft view, appeared plaufible enough; but on the other hand, it behoved me to weigh every circumftance before I placed too firm a confidence in this man's reports: By too implicit a faith, I might in a moment lofe the whole fruits of my voyage, perhaps be maffacred.

I well knew the intriguing fpirit of the half-bred Natives; this was but the acquaintance of a day, and confequently might be fufpected; a glafs of Brandy had
already

already rendered him a traitor, he appeared a friend to the Caffrees, had paffed his life among them, and came now from a retreat, where, perhaps, he had only refided for the purpofe of obferving the motions of the Colonifts, the better to betray them; might he not have an inclination to facrifice me alfo, in order to divide the booty with the Caffrees, and to gain their favour by leading me into the fnare?

After being agitated by a thoufand different ideas, I formed, what appeared to me, an eafy and fafe plan, which would give me time for reflection, and neither endanger my perfon or property; this was to fend a deputation to King Pharoo.

On the firft overture of this expedient Hans accepted the commiffion, which I took for a mark of honefty, and he promifed to perfuade two or three of his friends to accompany him in this expedition,

tion. I likewife purpofed fending two of my Hottentots (Adams and S nger) they were to give the King an account of all my proceedings for the laft eleven months, fince I quitted the Cape.

By this information he might conclude that curiofity alone conducted me into his territories. I alfo charged my meffengers to fay,—"That born in another world, a total ftranger to this country, I could not in any manner be the friend or accomplice of the Colonifts; on the contrary, I highly difapproved their conduct; in a word, they might be affured that as long as I remained in his country, I fhould give him no caufe of complaint, by any of my actions or proceedings, as I was actuated by the moft innocent motives, namely, to take a view of the country, and collect natural curiofities; and fo far from creating diforders, I fhould, on the contrary, take every occafion to be ufeful to himfelf
and

and subjects, as I had already been to several Hoords of Hottentots, who trusting to my honour had accepted my services; I added, that I should on my return to the Cape, render a faithful account to the Governor of all I had seen, and exert myself to the utmost in order to establish peace and harmony between them and the Colonists."

Having thus instructed my deputies, I charged my own Hottentots with a secret commission, which was, if possible, to bring back with them some Caffrees; this would enable me to judge what degree of confidence they reposed in my assurances, and likewise how far I might trust to them.

Nothing now remained but to stock themselves with provisions, this performed, I gave them some presents for the Caffrarian Prince; they bade me farewell, promising to return to *Koks-Kraal*, as soon as possible, where I was to wait their arrival.

Next morning we continued our journey, and after three hours march arrived on the borders of the river *Groot-Vis*. The heat was exceffive, and the earth covered with large round pebbles, which rendered the way very wearifome to my cattle; we kept on by the river-fide, 'till at length fatigue obliged us to ftop, though no later than four o'clock.

While the ufual preparations were making for our fecurity, I walked on the banks of the river, not far from which I perceived the remains of a Kraal of Caffrees. I was curious to examine it, and found fome huts in good prefervation, others intirely deftroyed, but a more melancholy fpectacle foon ftruck my attention, there was a number of human bones, which, from their appearance, I judged muft have lain a long time, and perhaps belonged to the unhappy people who were the firft victims of this unjuft war.

The

The night of the tenth paſſed in tolerable tranquillity, though ſome Hyænas approached our incampment, but being pretty much accuſtomed to their viſits, we ſuſtained but little uneaſineſs.

In the morning my Hottentots (who had been to fetch water) informed me they had diſcovered the recent tracks of Hippopotamuſes and *Coudous*. Our proviſions growing ſcarce, I determined to give this day to the chace; I therefore ſent my people to the banks of the river to diſcover if poſſible, the retreat of theſe animals; I went a different way, in hopes of finding Coudous, or other game, but ſaw only Gazells and Oſtriches, and being on foot, it was impoſſible to approach them.

I began now to think we ſhould have no ſport, when paſſing a plain where the graſs was high, and interſperſed with thickets, I ſuddenly perceived a group of

ſeven

seven *Coudous*, who fortunately did not see us. I approached with great precaution, followed by the man I had brought with me; being within two hundred feet, I ordered him to fire first, wishing to reserve my charge 'till they were upon the run. The report of my man's piece put them all to flight; by good fortune they passed within thirty paces of me, I fired, and shot the only male among them. My Hottentot would fain have persuaded me he had wounded it, but on examination we found only one ball had taken place; having covered him with some branches, I tied my handkerchief on a stick which we stuck in the ground, to frighten away the beasts of prey.

As I knew the females would not wander far without the male, we continued the pursuit, and soon after discovered a track of blood, which assured us another was wounded, and at the distance of about four hundred feet, we found it dying.

My Hottentot, whom I had accufed of awkwardnefs, was pleafed with the rencontre, though he aimed at the male and ftruck the female by chance. We fkinned and took out the intrails, by which means it was fo much lightened that we were able to carry and place it by the male.

Harraffed with fatigue and hunger, we made a fire, and broiled fome of the liver. I know not whether it was the excellence of the meat, or the fharpnefs of my appetite, but without feafoning or bread (of which I had not eaten a confiderable time) I thought it one of the greateft dainties I had ever tafted.

When we had finifhed our repaft, my Hottentot went to fetch two horfes and fome of his comrades, who carried our provifion to the camp. The kettles were all filled in an inftant; in the mean time they broiled fteakes on the coals, and in lefs.

less than two hours three parts of our meat disappeared.

The Hottentots are gluttons while they have plenty of provisions, at other times they are satisfied with little. In this particular they resemble the Hyæna, and indeed all carnivorous animals, who hastily devour their prey without a thought of the future, though they may possibly be some days before they get a fresh supply of food, appeasing their hunger in the interval with a kind of *Terre Glaise* (Potter's Clay) The Hottentot can eat in one day ten or twelve pounds of meat, but when this is not to be procured, Locusts, a Honey-Comb, or a piece of the leather of his sandals will serve to alleviate the pressing calls of hunger.

I could never make my people comprehend that it was prudent to reserve something for another day, for after having eat to the degree of excefs already recited, they would give the remainder to any chance comers; nor did this prodigality appear to give them the leaft concern. "We fhall hunt, (they faid) or we fhall fleep," — for fleep is to them a capital refource in times of need, and I never paffed any of the dry or fterile countries, where game is fcarce, without finding whole Hoords afleep in their Kraals, which is a certain affurance of their being in a miferable fituation; but what is furprifing, (and which I fhould not have affirmed but on repeated experience) they fleep at will, by this means deceiving or at leaft alleviating the moft preffing calls of nature.

They have, notwithftanding, their hours of wakefulnefs, which even cuftom cannot conquer, but they then make ufe of an expedient to prevent fleep, which will fcarcely appear probable, though ftrictly true: they bind the ftomach tight with a leather

leather girdle, by this means supporting or diminishing hunger. These bandages are likewise a general remedy amongst them, in almost all cases, binding the head or any other suffering part, and supposing that pain is to be expelled by violent pressure; having been often present on these occasions, I have ever observed that when the operation was finished, the patient appeared eased; strange as this may appear, it would not be so generally adopted, did it not, in some measure, answer the intended purpose.

The Hottentots that I had sent to discover the Hippopotimus, soon returned informing me, that in coasting the side of the river, they had discovered one in a place intirely covered with reeds; that each time it rose, they had heard it distinctly, and had fired at it several times, in order to frighten, and make it shift its situation; that probably by the next morning it might

might be in a place more favorable to our defigns; they had met likewife with twenty buffalos, but had not killed any.

The eleventh, at night, we were vifited by lions, hyænas and jackals, which kept us on the watch 'till two o'clock in the morning; the fmell of our frefh meat and cookery, no doubt, had attracted them. We had much trouble with our horfes, particularly that I bought of Mr. Mulder, in the canton of Auteniquas; the howling of the wild beafts frightened him fo much, that we were obliged to put clogs on each leg, and confine his head with a ftrap, to prevent his beating himfelf to pieces.

Tranquillity returned with the day, when we finifhed cutting up the Coudous; after which we packed our baggage.— I had fent a man the night before to view *Koks-Kraal*, which was the rendezvous appointed

appointed for my deputies, who had been gone but three days, so that I could not expect them for some time.

From the report of my messenger, I judged we might encamp very commodiously at this place, and the first view of that pleasing spot convinced me I was not mistaken. We reached it in three hours, and found an inclosure of about fifty feet square, formed by a hedge of dry branches and thorns; it was broken in some places, which we repaired in the course of the day. This enclosure was a fortunate circumstance, as it sheltered our beasts; and the spot was in so elevated a situation, that it overlooked all the environs.

On one side was a river, at only the distance of four hundred paces, which supplied us with plenty of water. This was not only a place of security from wild beasts, but also, in some measure, from the
Caffrees,

Caffrees, who being spread about the country, and uninformed of my pacific intentions, might, if we had been quite exposed, have fallen upon us unawares; but I was most apprehensive of my ambassador, who knowing perfectly the number of men I had with me, and informed of the precise spot for our meeting, might corrupt my Hottentots, or betray and assassinate them on the road; then returning at the head of a numerous party, by one of those strokes too common in war, exterminate me and my people.

I shall not hide from my readers, that filled with the idea of selling my life as dear as possible, my terrors increased in proportion to the care I took to defend it; but after my deputies had been absent some time, I became easier, the danger seemed to diminish, and at length I was wholly familiarized to my situation.

I ordered my large tent to be erected beyond the fence, at one end of our inclofure, furrounding it with fham huts, as we had before contrived at the river *Klin-Vis*. At an angle oppofite the tent we made a divifion for the horfes, and another for the fheep and goats, near which I placed my fmall tent, determined to fleep there. We furrounded the whole fo well with a fence of thorny bufhes, that it was impoffible any wild beafts could penetrate it, by which means my flocks were in perfect fafety in our little fortrefs, which alfo, in time of need, might ferve as a retreat for myfelf and people; and from whence we might have braved two thoufand Caffrees.

Thefe arrangements fatisfied my companions, who were yet more uneafy than myfelf. On the approach of night, at fifty paces diftant, we made large fires, to fcare the lions; we likewife had others nearer.

nearer. All thefe precautions anfwering perfectly well, I returned to my ufual occupations, and my people regained their cheerfulnefs.

I faw flights of parroquets in the air, and fhot one of a fpecies that has not yet been defcribed. It is about the fize of the grey parrot of Guinea; its colour green, of feveral fhades; on each leg, and on the joints of the wings, a bright aurora colour; but I fhall give a particular defcription of this in my hiftory of birds.

During the day we were ufually vifited by confiderable numbers of bavian monkeys, of the fame fpecies as my friend Kees; thefe animals appeared aftonifhed at feeing fo many people, and yet more fo, on perceiving one of their kind among us, who anfwered them in their own language. One day more than three hundred defcended from a hill, which was on the fide of our camp, and furrounded us, fcreaming *Gou-a-cou, Gou-a-cou*; the voice and appearance of Kees feeming to embolden them. They were not equal in fize, fome being much larger than others, but all of the fame fpecies; fkipping and gamboling in a manner difficult to be defcribed. An idea of thefe monkies fhould not be formed from thofe who languifh out a wearifome life of flavery in Europe; perifhing by the kindnefs of the ladies, or poifoned by their ill-beftowed dainties. The heavinefs of our atmofphere deadens their natural gaiety, and they frequently play anticks more from a dread of punifhment, than from real humour.

A fingularity that I have before remarked, fixed my attention; it was, that Kees, whom I held by the paw, though he appeared to know and anfwer his fellows, would by no means come near them; I pulled him forward, the ftrange animals (who

(who simply appeared to stand on their guard) waited my approach, with as much tranquillity as Kees shewed agitation and resistance. On a sudden he escaped, and ran to hide himself in my tent; perhaps a fear that they would drag him with them, caused his uneasiness.

The other monkies continued their antic gambols and screams for some time; 'till tired with the noise, and weary of the fight, I fired my piece; in an instant the dogs were at their heels. It was now really amusing to see the dexterity and quickness of their flight; dispersing in every direction; leaping from rock to rock, and disappearing with the rapidity of lightning.

CHAP. XXI.

THE AUTHOR ENDEAVOURS TO DISCOVER SOME HIPPOPOTAMUSES — PART OF HIS PEOPLE PURSUED BY LIONS — OBSERVATIONS ON WILD BEASTS.

ON the thirteenth day of the month I was awakened by a bird, whose note was extremely loud and distinct, but resembled nothing I had ever before heard. I rose immediately, and got very near without its discovering me; but being hardly day light, I could not distinguish it among the thick branches on which

which it was perched, and, in the end, had the misfortune to lose it. From its flight I took it for the *Crapaud Volant* (Flying Toad) I was not mistaken, for some days after I shot several.

This bird is very different from the Crapaud Volant of Europe, whose note is only a plaintive cry, like the ground toad, which has probably procured it this name: that of Africa warbles very articulately, and in a manner not to be imitated; continuing for hours after sun-set, and sometimes all night. This difference, joined to its outward texture, proves it of another species.

I killed several birds, among others a small kind of *Barbu*, hitherto unknown; and a cuckoo, which I named the cryer, as his piercing note may be heard at a great distance, but does not at all resemble that of our European cuckoo; its plumage is likewise very different.

I also found in this canton, several of the golden cuckoos, described by Buffon, by the name of *Coucou Vert Doré*, of the Cape; this bird is, without dispute, the most beautiful of its kind, white, green and gold, enrich its plumage; perched on the highest trees, it warbles continually, with varied modulation, the syllables, *Di Di Didric*, as distinctly as I have written them, for which reason I named it the *Didric*.

As I was amusing myself in pursuing some small birds, I discovered a flight of crows and vultures, rising and circling in the air, and making a violent noise.—— When I had arrived nearly under them, I discovered the remains of a buffalo, that had been devoured by a lion, apparently about twenty-four hours since. From the aspect of the field of battle, I judged the combat to have been terrible; the ground was beaten, and in places torn up; I could

I could difcover by the marks, how many times the buffalo had fallen; and in places lay tufts of the lion's hair, which his opponent had torn off with his feet or horns.

I was not far from the river, where I difcovered frefh tracks of the Hippopotamus; I followed them, and difcovered where they had regained the water.——Though very attentive, I could hear no noife; the bufhes and reeds prevented my reaching the edge of the river, and compleatly hid the animals.

It was near dinner time, I was fatigued and fafting; the Crapaud Volant and other birds had led me a good diftance.—I was returning to my camp the neareft way, confulting the fun and directing my courfe eaftward; when I was ftartled by a gun that was fired almoft clofe to me; as it was totally unexpected. I knew it muft must proceed from some of my men, and ran to the spot, where I found one of the worst markſmen waſting my powder. He informed me he had been watching a Hippopotamus ever ſince day-break; that he had juſt fired, and no doubt killed it. An aukward hand may ſometimes have a fortunate ſtroke, and though I knew the animal would not riſe under a full quarter of an hour, I determined to wait, ſending the Hottentot for part of my men, and ſome proviſion. After an hour and half's impatient waiting, my people arrived; but our prey had not yet made its appearance. The Hottentot aſſured me, that after he had fired the animal plunged into the water, and that he had remarked quantities of blood on the ſurface; he added, as the currant was very ſtrong, the Hippopotamus might have been carried along with the ſtream, which I thought poſſible; my man therefore departed, in hopes of meeting it lower down the river, while

while I returned to the camp, to prepare my birds.

About one o'clock we had a dreadful ftorm, the thunder fell feveral times in the foreft that bordered the mountains. One of my men returned with a gazell he had fhot. The Hottentot who fired at the Hippopotamus came home late, without having feen any more of it, and was obliged to meet the farcafms of my Hottentot wits, who tried to perfuade him he had fired at a *Legouane* (a kind of large lizard, common in the rivers of Africa.) Pleafantries at length gave way to abufe, and my epigramifts were on the point of concluding by a boxing bout.—With a word I ended the difpute, and filenced the orators.

On the fourteenth the rain fell abundantly in the night, and extinguifhed our fires, fo that we could not re-light them.

The

The dogs made such a perpetual barking, that it was impossible to sleep; notwithstanding we heard no wild beasts. I have before observed, that on rainy nights, the lion, tiger and hyæna never make a noise, which redoubles the danger; for they continue ranging, and fall unawares on their prey. What added to the fright, occasioned by a knowledge of this circumstance, was, that the damp prevented the dogs from scenting. My men were so aware of the danger, that when the rain had extinguished the fires, it was with the utmost difficulty they could be persuaded to try to light them.

It must be allowed, that stormy nights in the African desarts, present a powerful image of desolation and horror, and involuntarily strike the mind with terror. When these deluges fall, they soon overflow and run through tents, mats, and every thing in their passage; the repeated flashes

flashes of lightning, giving twenty times in a minute fearful glances of flaming light, instantly contrasted by the most dreadful obscurity. The continued and almost deafening claps of thunder refounding from all parts, and meeting with horrible crash, echo from mountain to mountain, multiplying the horrors of the scene. The moans of domestic animals, moments of dismal silence, all concur to render these times truly dreadful. The danger of attack from wild beasts adds to the general panic, which only the return of light, and subsiding of the storm, can dispel.

Day broke, but it was gloomy, and charged with clouds, the rain falling at intervals; I was not disposed to go out, but employed myself in taking a review of my birds, and recently-prepared collection. I had enough to fill a chest, which I did with great care, caulking and lining

lining it in my usual manner, to prevent the intrusion of insects. On a general recapitulation of those I now possessed, and those I had sent from the country of Auteniquas, I found the number amounted to about seven hundred.

Towards four o'clock in the afternoon the sky cleared, which revived our fainting courage, and we returned to our accustomed exercises. I sometimes made my Hottentots shoot at a mark, this always gave them great pleasure, which I frequently indulged, as by these means they greatly improved, and I had remarked from the beginning, that their courage augmented with their skill; while they received as a favor, what I granted in a political view, for the safety of my caravan.

The prize was usually a portion of tobacco; a bottle stuck against a rock served for

for a mark, and the conditions required to break it at a diftance of two hundred and fifty feet. It was one named Pit who fucceeded this time, on the fifty-fourth fhot. I gave him the prize, which he generoufly fhared with his companions. The balls were not loft by this amufement, as we ever found them near the foot of the rock.

The fetting fun feemed to promife a fine morning, I determined therefore to hunt the Hippopotamus, and for that purpofe fent feveral of my men to the banks of the river, to obferve if they could difcover any. We cleaned all our fire-arms, and caft large balls, in which (according to the African cuftom) I put an eighth part of pewter; the balls by this means penetrate farther, as they do not flatten againft the bones.

After

After the evening fires were kindled (a task which was not easily accomplished, as the ground was damp, and the wood wet.) I regaled my men with tea, and I am certain, that over one ounce they poured at least fifty pints of boiling water.

The evening was one of the most amusing we had yet past; ever some joke, pun, or pleasant tale, from these good folks, who seated round the fire, endeavoured to amuse me, and fix my attention, by giving proofs of attachment and cordiality.

Above all, the question was, who should shew the most prowess the next day, in chace of the Hippopotamus; all wished to be there, and this made it difficult to settle the party to the general satisfaction. I wished some of my men to distribute themselves about the country, to shoot gazells,

gazells, on which I built more for provision than on the Hippopotamufes, particularly as the edge of the river was fo covered with reeds, bufhes and trees, that it **was** difficult to find them.

As night advanced I was furprized the men I fent on difcovery were not returned; I ordered three guns to be fired; near half an hour paffed without any anfwer, when at intervals of four or five minutes, we diftinguifhed three reports, which made us judge they were pointed at an Hippopotamus. In a quarter of an hour we heard three more difcharges; but the found did not appear fo diftant as before. From time to time the firing continued, each report founding nearer, which perfuaded us the unhappy men were flying from fome wild beaft. I ufed my utmoft fpeed to join them, directed by the guns; at length they appeared, alarmed and trembling, but had feen nothing; though

from

from the uneafinefs of the two dogs they had with them, they were convinced fome lions purfued their fteps. The dogs, as we afterwards found had not deceived them.

The Hottentots informed me they had heard the grunting of an Hippopotamus, rather above the fpot, where they had laid wait; this information pleafed me, but we wanted reft, and returned to the camp.

About half paft eleven, the roaring of a lion, at a very fmall diftance, ftruck my ear, which was immediately anfwered by another of the fame fpecies, but confiderably further off; but this laft joined the other in a quarter of an hour, and together they kept ranging round the camp. We were foon prepared for them, and making a general difcharge of our pieces, intimidated, and forced the animals to fly. I had no doubt they were the fame that had followed

followed my men the night before, who certainly owed their safety to the information given by the dogs.

It would be difficult to express how very fearful the boldest dog is of a Lion, and it is easy during the night, to discover by his countenance, what species of wild beast is near. If a Lion, the dog, without stirring, begins to howl fearfully, and experiencing the greatest uneasiness, creeps towards the human species, and caressing him, seems to demand protection. The other domestic animals are not less agitated, all rising, none attempting to sleep. The oxen lowing in an under melancholy tone; Horses paw and suffer great agitation; the Goats, likewise, shew their alarm, and the sheep pressed one against another, form an immovable mass——Man alone, proud and sanguine, seizes his weapon, and palpitating with impatience, sighs to meet his victim.

On

On these occasions, the alarm of Kees was very striking; fearful of our guns as of the approach of the Lion, the smallest movement made him tremble; moaning as if sick, he kept close by my side, dragging after me, as though overpowered with deadly weakness. The Cock alone appeared astonished at the common agitation, a Spar-Hawk would have thrown him into consternation, and he dreaded the smell of a Pole-Cat more than all the Lions of Africa. Thus it is, that each has a dreaded enemy, man only, dares all, fears none, except his own species.

We sometimes see wild animals of the same kind fighting, but love is the only passion that disunites them, and provokes their momentary quarrels, which are presently succeeded by peace. Among domestic animals, hatred is more durable; is this an effect of tuition or example?

I must return to the different ways by which danger is announced, and may without vanity affirm, that no one can more truly delineate them, as all the compilations of speculative eloquence can never equal observations, so often repeated on that extensive theatre, the deserts of Africa.

If an Hyæna approaches, the dog will pursue it within a certain distance, without any particular symptoms of fear. The Ox continues laying on the earth without alarm, except it is a young beast, that has never before heard that dangerous animal; the Horse remains without any apparent fear. If Jackals (a kind of Foxes) come near, the dogs pursue them with eagerness to a prodigious distance, unless they scent Lions or Hyænas by the way, in which case they return as quick as possible.

The Hottentots pretend that the Jackal is the spy of other beasts, that he comes to excite and provoke the dogs to follow him, that the Lion or Hyæna may have the better opportunity to seize on their prey, which they share amicably with him, in recompense for the service performed.

What I have seen may in some measure lead to this assertion, which is most likely exaggerated; it is certain that as soon as the Jackals begin their concert, the Lion or Hyæna is to be expected; these, however, will not shew themselves unless the dogs are engaged. We ever kept two tied up, to bark in the absence of the rest, and prevent the approach of the Hyæna, who fears fire less than the Lion.

CHAP.

CHAP. XXI.

KILLS A HIPPOPOTAMUS — ACCOUNT OF THAT ANIMAL — A VULGAR ERROR CONTRADICTED RESPECTING THE EAGLE.

ON the morrow, which was the fifteenth, we were all on foot at day break, I sent three men to hunt for Buffaloes, Gazells, Gnous, and Coudous; I then took four of my best marksmen with three Hottentots to carry my large carbine, ammunition, and some dried provisions, in case we should be obliged to pass the day in the field, and leaving the rest of my people with Scanepoel to take care of the camp, we departed

In coasting the river, we approached the banks as near as possible, keeping a profound silence. We walked three hours in this manner, without making any discovery, but at length saw the foot marks of a Hippopotamus, and followed the track for an hour and half, which conducted us to the spot from whence it took to the water. On our separating to watch along the banks, the man who was farthest off fired his piece, but his shot did not take effect.

We did not wait long before it rose again to breathe, with the head intirely out of the water; the animal having now gained the opposite shore of the river, which was very wide, two of my people swam over, in hopes to oblige it at least to keep the middle, if they could not get it nearer;

nearer; thus far the scheme answered, but the Hippopotamus shewed so much distrust, hardly putting its nose out of the water, and changing its situation every moment, never coming up in the same place, and replunging so suddenly, that it was impossible to take any certain aim, having already fired thirty times without effect.

The Hottentots that passed the river had no guns, the cunning animal remarked the fire did not come from that side, and therefore kept pretty near the shore.

I now ordered Pit (the man who won the last prize) to pass the river out of sight of the Hippopotamus, and join his companions, but not to fire without being sure of his mark; and he executed these orders very punctually.

The animal thinking itself safe on the opposite side, shewed little distrust, lifting its head sometimes entirely out of the water. Pit watched his opportunity so well on this occasion, and directed his shot with such precision, that I made no doubt but the animal was severely wounded, by its rearing the major part of its body out of the water, and struggling violently. I immediately lodged a ball in the breast, on which it disappeared for twenty minutes, after which we perceived it dead, and driving with the current; some of my people now plunged into the river and conducted it to shore.

I shall not attempt to paint the general joy, on seeing this monstrous animal in our possession, but our motives were very different; gluttony presented it to my people as a dainty, on which they were soon to gorge; while curiosity offered it to me as an interesting object of Natural History, and which I yet knew only from books and engravings,

The

The legs of the Hippopotamus are short in proportion to its size, which was an advantage to us, as we could roll it on the ground like a German-tun, being equally round. I could not for a long time help admiring and examining this enormous beast; it was a female; the ball from Pit had taken place above the left eye, and stuck in the jaw; I much doubt whether that wound would have been mortal. My shot had entered the shoulder, perforated the lungs, and broke a rib.

This animal measured, from the tip of the nose to the tail, ten feet seven inches, and eight feet eleven inches in circumference, its bent tusks were more than five inches long, and one in diameter in the thickest part, which made me conjecture it was young; in the stomach were leaves and reeds grosly chewed, likewise small branches of the size of a goose-quill, which appeared only a little flattened, and I have remarked that large animals, such as the Elephant and Rhinoceros masticate their food very little.

All engravings of the Hippopotamus are very imperfect, the best I know of, is (without contradiction) that of Mr. Allaman, Professor of Physic, at Leyden, which was engraved from drawings he received from Mr. Gordon. In my description of animals I shall have one copied that I drew myself, and which I hope will satisfy the naturalist.

I sent a Hottentot to the camp, with orders to bring the next morning two sets of oxen, to carry home our prize, and as it was late, we chose a large tree, under which we determined to pass the night. It was near the river, and within sight of the animal, which we durst not quit for fear of its being visited by carnivorous beasts; we were surrounded by trees, which

rendered

rendered our situation critical, as we might have been surprised; but by lighting large fires, and at stated intervals discharging our pieces, we passed the night in safety, though it was not possible to sleep for gnats, who, attracted by the neighbourhood of the water, and the coolness of the spot we had chosen, swarmed round us by miriads; one of my men who slept, had his face so much stung and swelled that he was hardly to be known.

I took care to have a foot of the Hippopotamus prepared in the same manner as that of the first Elephant I had killed, five months before, in my way to *Ange-Kloof*.

The foot (which had been dressing all night) was served up for my breakfast, and I thought it superior to the Elephant's, never having eat any thing with greater satisfaction.

Though

Though the Hippopotamus is extremely fat, it is not of so disgusting a quality as that of other animals; my people melted and sipped it by porringers full, like broth; they likewise anointed themselves in such a manner, that they appeared as if varnished all over; their excess in eating and greasing having made their skins tighten and shine to a degree which proved they had not been very frugal in the use of it.

I had forgot to send for a horse, but Swanepoel thought for me; the heat was extreme, and we were six good leagues from the camp. I ordered the Hippopotamus to be fastened to a chain, to which we harnassed twelve oxen. While we continued our way by the river side, they experienced great difficulty and fatigue from the roughness of the road, and from trees that perpetually intercepted our passage, but as soon as we reached the plain, which was covered with high grass, I caused the oxen

to

to be changed, and seeing the second set went on well, mounted my horse and made the best of my way to the camp. Gager, my favorite dog, who never quitted me in all my parties, was this time obliged to lag behind with the Hottentots, who arrived about five o'clock in the evening.

The three Hottentots I had sent in search of game, also returned fortunate, having killed two Gnous and three Gazells, which abundantly supplied us with provisions; but the excessive heat, and dragging the Hippopotamus on the ground, had bruised it so much, that some of the best part began to spoil, which obliged us to pass the night in cutting up and salting a part of it, which we put in the skins of the Gnous my men had killed, reserving the best pieces to pack in a brandy barrel, having first secured the liquor in pitchers, My men did not let slip this opportunity to get very drunk.

The

The following night our two lions returned, accompanied by several hyænas and jackals. One of the hyænas was bold enough to pass our fires, and approach us; on which a Hottentot fired, but missed her. The jackals too came into our camp; and had it not been for our dogs, we must have shared our provisions with them.

The next day my men employed themselves in cutting the skin off the Hippopotamus, to make what, in this country, the call *Chanboc*, which are whips, used to drive the oxen. They are like those used in Europe, but much larger and longer. The skin, which in some parts is two inches thick, is cut into proper lengths, of two inches wide, which renders it an exact square; they make each piece about six feet long, tie a weight to one end, hang it up to dry, and afterwards beat and round it with a mallet, making it gradually

gradually smaller towards one end. They form less ones for horses, which have the peculiar advantage **over those of** Europe of never breaki**ng, especially** if sometimes rubbed with a little oil.

They make the same use of the skins of the Rhinoceros; these **indeed are prefered** by the inhabitants **of the** Cape, for though not so strong, they receive a finer polish, **being almost** as transparent as horn; but **the Colonists, prefering utility** to beauty, ever use the former. These whips are dear, as neither of the animals from which they are made, are now to be procured in the Colonies; and, frequently, **those** who go further in search of **them,** are disappointed, by not meeting with any.

The skin of these animals is not fit for any other use; it is much like that of the hog, **except in thickness;** indeed the

Hippo-

Hippopotamus, in some measure, resembles that animal; there is little difference in the fat, and if it could be salted with requisite precaution, it would be prefered; especially as it is reckoned extremely salutary. At the Cape, for instance, the fat is thought so wholesome, that they affirm, if it is taken in regular portions, it will radically cure all disorders of the breast. I kept some by me that was not thicker than the oil of olives in the coldest weather.

The tusks of the Hippopotamus are of a superior quality to ivory; the latter growing yellow by time, while the former preserves its original purity and whiteness; no wonder therefore, that the Europeans make them so great an object of traffic, particularly the French, as by the aid of art they supplant nature, and figure admirably in the mouth of a pretty woman.

My

My Hottentots reckoned on a second hunt of the Hippopotamus, their feasting on the first being yet fresh in their memories; but I found we had provision enough, and that our time might be more usefully employed, or at least, that we might vary our occupations, and therefore determined to try fishing.

With some difficulty I found a place on the river proper for my net; our success was not great, we only caught about twenty fish, of two or three kinds, the longest of which was not above six inches; but fried in the fat of the Hippopotamus they were excellent.

This fishing was not considerable enough to interest us, particularly as the approach to the river was rather difficult and disagreeable, we therefore drew out our net. While they were folding it, a bird approached ed us without any sign of fear, uttering a shrill cry.

My men said it was a bird that discovers honey, and I observed it bore a great analogy to one, known to ornithologists, by the name of the *Coucou Indicateur* (Indicative Cuckoo;) but this was much larger than the bird already known to me. The Hottentots are very fond of it, on account of the service it renders them, they therefore begged me to spare its life; but as it was of a new species, which I wished to join to my collection, I could not resist the inclination of shooting it.

I found it was of the species of Indicative Cuckoos already known, but larger, with some difference in the plumage.—Some time after I killed three birds of this kind, who differed from each other, though of the same species.

They

They are well known to the natives of Africa, who hold them in great respect; they live entirely on honey and wax, which they involuntarily discover. The naturalists place this bird (though I know not why) among the cuckoos, which it only resembles in the formation of its feet; being quite different in every other respect.

I perhaps may run the risk of being censured by possessors of scientific cabinets; but I cannot avoid saying, that large volumes are nothing compared with the great book of nature; and though an error may have been strengthened by a hundred eloquent pens, it is, notwithstanding, yet an error.

This bird has no more similarity to the cuckoo than the wood-pecker, *barbus*, paroquet, and a number of others, whose feet are alike. If it must be ranged in a
known

known clafs, it appertains more to the barbus, which it moft refembles.

In the ftomach of this bird I found nothing but wax, and fome honey, not the leaft appearance of any infects. The fkin is thick, and of fo clofe a texture, that even when frefh, it can hardly be pierced with a pin; which I confider as one of nature's admirable precautions, for having deftined this bird to difpute its fubfiftence with the moft ingenious of infects, fhe has alfo afforded a covering which the fting cannot penetrate.

It builds its neft in the hollows of trees, climbing like the wood-pecker, and fits upon its own eggs; this little account of its manners is fufficient to feparate it totally from the cuckoo, and diftinguifh it as a different kind.

My Hottentot Klaas, in returning from hunting, brought an eagle which he had killed, it was of a species unknown to me, and undescribed by any author; I recompenced him, and gave him likewise a double quantity of tobacco; not that I was more generous to Klaas on this occasion than I should have been to another, though I prefered him to the rest, but I wished to excite, in my people, a desire of making discoveries.

This bird was extremely black, and seemed to resemble the vulture as much as the eagle, though different in some instances. Hunger changes the eagle into a vulture, that is to say, when distressed for food it will feed on putrified carrion. It is a vulgar error, that this bird only subsists by preying on others; for when I caused the offal of animals we had killed to be spread about, to attract carnivorous birds, eagles,

eagles, as well as others, profited by the carnage.

I here aſk pardon of the ancient and modern poets, for thus degrading the nature of this noble king of birds; for I muſt call it degrading, to ſee this favorite bird of Jove feeding on the ſcattered remains of infected carrion.

CHAP. XXII.

VISIT OF THE GONAQUAIS—ARE ENTERTAINED BY THE AUTHOR—MEETS WITH NARINA—DEPARTURE OF THE HOORD.

ON the eighteenth we paſſed great part of the night in firing our pieces, to drive away the lions, who continued to viſit us, as did alſo the voracious hyænas, which prevented my ſleeping 'till very late. When I awoke in the morning I was much ſurpriſed to find myſelf ſurrounded by twenty Gonaquias. But this viſit deſerves the moſt ample deſcription, from which the reader may form a better judgment of thefe favages, than by all the laboured difcourfes of philofophy.

The chief approached firft, to make his compliments; the women followed, decorated to the utmoft, frefh greafed, and powdered with *Boughcu* (or Bucku;) this is a red duft, made from a root of that name, with which they powder their fkins after being greafed, and which is tolerably agreeable; in addition to this, their faces were all painted in a hundred different forms. Each made me a prefent—one gave me oftriches eggs, another a young lamb, others offered me milk in bafkets, a circumftance that aftonifhed me.—— "What!" exclaimed I, "milk in bafkets!" I recollected at that moment the difgufting copper veffels, which fome time fince were ufed for milk in Paris, 'till they were forbid by the wifdom of the police; and in comparing them with thofe of the Gonaquais,

naquais, I could not help reflecting, how often a powerful city, with all its arts, palaces and great men, is distanced by the simple productions of those it may despise.

These baskets are very pretty, and fabricated with reeds, so closely interwoven, that they will hold water, and were afterwards of much service to me for that use; the Gonaquai chief informed me they were made by the Caffrees, from whom they had procured them.

The chief, who was named Haabas, presented me with a fine plume of ostrich feathers; and to shew how much I honoured his present, I took out those that were in my hat, and put his in the place. Satisfaction now marked the features of the good old man, and his words and gestures plainly evinced how much he was pleased with the compliment.

It was now time to shew I was neither unmindful nor ungrateful for these favors; I therefore began, by presenting him with several pounds of tobacco; this procured me, at a small expence, a scene of the most interesting nature. Haabas, by a sign, assembled all his people, who forming a circle, squatted down on the ground; and I saw, with infinite satisfaction, the chief distribute the tobacco among them, reserving only an equal portion for himself.

The spirit of equity which shone so brightly in this good man, excited my admiration; and I added to my former present (for his own use) a knife, a steel, a box of tinder, and a necklace of large glass beads. To the women I gave necklaces, and brass wire for bracelets.

In the midst of these reciprocal offerings of friendship, I remarked a young girl of about

about sixteen, who shewed less eagerness to partake of the ornaments I bestowed on her companions, than to consider my person; she examined me with such marked attention, that I drew near, to satisfy her curiosity. Her figure was charming, her teeth beautifully white, her height and shape, elegant and easy, and might have served as a model for the pencil of Albane; in short, she was the youngest sister of the graces, under the figure of a female Hottentot.

The force of beauty is universal, 'tis a sovereign whose power is unlimited. I felt by the prodigality of my presents, that I paid some deference to its power. The young savage and myself were soon acquainted. I gave her a girdle, bracelets, and a necklace of small white beads, which appeared to delight her; I then took a red handkerchief from my neck, with which she bound her head, in this dress she was
charming;

charming! I took pleasure in decorating her, which finished, she asked me for ornaments for her sister, who had remained at home; she pointed out to me her mother, told me she had no father. Nothing could equal the pleasure I took in seeing her, except it was in hearing her speak, for I was so charmed with her answers, that I fatigued her with interrogations. I asked her to stay with me, making her all sorts of promises; but when I spoke of carrying her to my country, where women I told her, were all queens, commanding Hoords of slaves; she rejected my proposal, and even gave marks of impatience and ill-humour. A monarch could not have prevailed on her to quit her Hoord and family, the bare idea inspired her with melancholy, to banish which, I changed the subject, and desired her to bring her sister, which she promised to do. Then fixing her eyes on a chair, shewed me a knife that laid there: I presented her with it; this she carried to her mother.

She was fully employed with her new decorations; examining her arms, feet, necklace and girdle, twenty times feeling her head, and adjusting her handkerchief, with which she appeared much pleased. I set my glass before her, she viewed herself very attentively, and even with complacency, shewing by her gestures how much she was satisfied, not particularly with her person, but her ornaments.

On her departure from the Hoord in the morning, to visit me, her cheeks had been rubbed with grease and soot; I made her wash it off, but could never persuade her that these decorations diminished rather than increased her beauty, and whatever skill I used in my persuasions, she still remained as obstinately attached to her filthy grease, as in our climates, the ladies are to rouge and pastes, which though not less disgusting are more pernicious.

My

My charming pupil defired me to give her my looking-glafs, I confented; fhe made good ufe of the empire her gentlenefs had acquired, to afk for all that gave her pleafure, notwithftanding I was obliged to deny her feveral things that were particularly ufeful to me, and might have been dangerous to her. My knee buckles had tempted her—the moft fparkling gems were not fo brilliant as her expreffive eyes. I fhould have been delighted to have given them. How much did I wifh at that moment for the moft miferable faftenings to fupply this ufelefs luxury! unhappily they were the only pair I poffeffed—I made her comprehend that the buckles were abfolutely neceffary to me, from which moment fhe never named them.

I found her name difficult to pronounce, difagreeable to the ear, and inapplicable to my ideas, I therefore re-named her *Narina*, which in the Hottentot language fignifies

a

MARIVA,
A Young Gonaquais.

a flower, desiring her to retain this name for my sake. She promised to keep it as long as she lived, in remembrance of me, and in testimony of her love; a sentiment that was no longer a stranger to her heart; this was truly painted in her gentle unadorned language, which powerfully shewed how strong the first impressions of nature are, and that even in the deserts of Africa there is no happiness without an alloy.

I ordered a sheep to be killed, and a good quantity of the Hippopotamus to be dressed, to regale our visitors, who gave into the excess of gaiety; every one danced, my Hottentots not to be out-done in gallantry, entertained them with music, sounding the *Goura*, the *Joum-Joum*, and the *Rabouquin*, nor was the *Jews-Harp* forgotten; this new instrument delighted our visitors. Narina, who thought (like all other pretty women) that she was capable of every thing, tried to play; to carry the likeness

likeness still farther, was soon tired of her lesson, and threw the instrument from her, calling it detestable.

The day passed in mirth and feasting; my men shared their brandy (besides what I had given myself) among our visitors. . I saw with pleasure that Narina could not drink; her sobriety delighted me—I detest liquors myself, and am amazed how women (particularly) can accustom themselves to the most disgusting of all poisons.

I reminded my people early of gathering wood for fires, which was soon performed; the Gonaquais were of the party, and amply provided for their own use. I permitted them to remain all night, assigning them a spot at some distance from the camp. Night approaching our fires were kindled, and I regaled my people with tea and coffee. Narina liked tea, but the colour of coffee disgusted her; I covered her eyes therefore

therefore with my hand, and got her to drink half a dish; she thought it good, but still preferred tea, drinking a great quantity which much amazed me, for notwithstanding her assertion, that she liked it, she seemed to drink the tea in haste, in order to reach the sugar at the bottom.

After this frugal meal they returned to dancing 'till midnight, when fatigue obliged them to retire to rest.

I had for some time slept in my waggon to avoid the night-dews, I therefore accommodated the Gonaquai chief with my tent. The reader no doubt supposes that Narina was not among those who were excluded my camp. She had no idea of quitting her friend, 'till I pointed out her mother and companions who were about to depart, when I received the adieu of the gentle Narina.

I sent two of my people armed to pass the night with the Gonaquais, and defend them, should any carnivorous beasts approach; when they were departed I ordered the rest of my people to rest.

I could not sleep myself, all that had passed since the arrival of the Gonaquais was painted on my imagination in new and pleasing colours; the manners of these people were so pure, simple and interesting, and so different from the account given by some romantic travellers. My conversation with Haabas and Narina, particularly pleased me, and made me think the time mis-spent in their absence, and the hours too rapid in their company.

In the morning I visited the camp of the Gonaquais, it was just day break, they all slept profoundly, rolled up in their Kroses, (these are cloaks, made of the skins of different animals, and serve for a covering both

both day and night) Narina was with her mother, on a mat I had given them; the seven other women were huddled together, and formed a laughable group; neither heads or feet were to be seen, but entirely concealed under their coverings. I bid them good morrow by firing my piece; on the instant their heads popped up, and exhibited the most comical picture imaginable; notwithstanding this noise some did not awake, which is not to be wondered at, as the sleep of the Hottentots is almost lethargic. I gave them time to recover their surprise, wishing to shoot some game before the heat of the day.

I returned about ten o'clock with some birds, and among others a Gobe Mouch, (Fly Catcher.) This charming bird is of a fine red, with a long tail, its head ornamented with a beautiful tuft of the same colour with the body, but brighter; the long feathers in the tail gave it an air of dignity;

dignity; this the female of the same species does not possess, nor does the male bird keep this distinction longer than pairing time, which lasts about three months, soon after which these two feathers drop, nothing then distinguishes it from the hen, but the darker shades of its plumage.

This bird must not be mistaken for one of the same species, described by Buffon, and Brisson, by the name of the tufted or long-tailed fly-catcher of the Cape; for this bird is not found there. That belongs to the Indies, and particularly to the Isle of Ceylon, and is very different from mine; the characters that particularly distinguish them will be given in my Ornithology, and I can only say before hand, that the birds described by that name, one of which is near white, the other red, and which are given as different species, are absolutely the same, and that the variety of colours arise from the difference of the seasons, which

any

any one may be convinced of, by examining one I have in my cabinet, who is immediately between the two ſtates, and ſhews clearly the progreſſion from white to red.

That I had juſt ſhot never experiences that change, which is enough to diſtinguiſh and rank it in a different claſs.

After carrying home my birds, I returned to the ſettlement of my viſitors; the men only were there, the women, I was informed, were gone to bathe. Curious to ſee this ceremony, I went to the river; their voices and laughter ſoon led me to the ſpot; I glided between the trees, and arrived on the banks without being ſeen. They were all ſwimming, playing and diving with admirable dexterity.

After having for ſome time obſerved the ſwimmers, I fired my gun, and preſented myself before them; they instantly plunged into the water, shewing only the tip of their noses. I seated myself on their habiliments, which were put together in a heap, tantalizing them, by holding these up, and inviting them to come and dress themselves. The mother of Narina laughed at the distress of her companions very heartily; she had quitted the water before my arrival, and was seated under a tree, waiting for the rest.

For a long time they intreated me to go, but I was deaf to their solicitation. At length they thought of a scheme, which was executed with a skill that astonished me. They knew of my partiality for Narina; her mother, therefore, threw her kros and apron to her, and she dressed herself in the water; then coming to me, with an air of supplicating tenderness, entreated me to retire, and give her companions time to dress. I pretended unwillingness,
but

but taking my hand, she succeeded, by half forcing me out of sight; at the same time calling to her friends to make haste and dress.

We then continued our way to the tent, Narina playing with me by the way, with as much freedom as if I had been her brother, or one of her companions; sometimes running and leaping over bushes, brooks and pits, that intercepted her passage. Being young and inured to fatigue, I might have set our European Herculeses at defiance; but whether the remains of gallantry made me exert but half my strength in opposition to Narina, or that she had greater skill and agility, I cannot tell, but I was generally obliged to yield her the palm of victory. Sometimes, getting a little forward, she would challenge me to race with her, then darting along with amazing swiftness, she would bound over the paths, and gaining the different turnings of of the wood, meet and furprife me in the paffage.

The different birds that were flying about in the foreft, obliged me often to ufe my gun; it was the only method I had to reftrain the wildnefs of my young favage; nothing could equal the pleafure fhe took in feeing me fire.

In our way I fhot twenty birds, and as I had no dog with me, Narina picked up the game. I had loft fight of my camp; the mirth and playfulnefs of my young companion having led me further than I intended: She concluded, however, with a retaliation for the trick I had ferved herfelf and companions, on the banks of the *Groot-Vis*.

In our walk we had again met with that river; a heron which I fhot fell in the water, and was carried by the current

rent into the middle of the ſtream; I ſhould have been particularly ſorry to have loſt it, having before taken great pains to procure one, which was ſpoiled by the negligence of my people.

I was for immediately plunging into the river, but was very much incommoded by the reeds and grafs which grew on the banks; Narina, who ſaw my embarraſſment, and how aukwardly I attemped to gain my bird, ruſhed into the river, and ſoon recovered the wiſhed-for prize. I ſtood on the bank, earneſtly inviting her to ſhore; but with a playful archneſs, ſhe turned a deaf ear to all my entreaties, holding up the bird, and beckoning me to fetch it. To provoke me the more, ſhe ſwam over to the oppoſite ſide, from whence ſhe made game of my cowardice. I have before obſerved I could not ſwim.

When

When I found I could not obtain the bird, I seated myself on the bank of the river, and waited patiently for her return; on perceiving this, she swam back, diving by the way as she crossed. I presented my piece in jest, which did not in the least alarm her; she only the more obstinately refused me the heron.———We now took the direct road to the camp.

The female Gonaquais, whom we had left on the borders of the river, soon joined us; a bashful shame was marked on their features, and gave me cause to blush for having sported with their delicacy.

I gave my savages their breakfasts, my dissecting table was already set out, this was used for no other purpose, and with two chairs formed the whole furniture of my tent. I now began preparing my birds. This was an operation they knew nothing of, and at which they seemed surprised.

prised, nor could they conceive why I first killed the birds, and then endeavoured to restore them to their natural forms. I did not lose time in explaining to them the nature and value of the cabinets collected by the curious; all this would have appeared too mysterious. But they would have been yet more astonished had I told them, that my travelling so far was principally for that purpose.

Narina once asked me if there were no birds in my country; it would have been vain to have entered into long dissertations on a subject that would not have been understood; besides, I was at that time busied in preparing a king-fisher, which I presented to my lively savage.

Haabas intreated me to place my camp near his Hoord, where I should find great variety of birds. He made me understand, that the distance was about two leagues;

leagues; and I promised to visit him in a few days.

They were now preparing to depart; I made them all dine with me; after which I gave Haabas a small quantity of tobacco, which much pleased him. Narina promised to bring me some milk, and to conduct her sister to the camp. At length, thoroughly satisfied with each other, and with often repeated adieus, the good people quitted me, I caused them to be accompanied by one of my people, whom I charged to learn the road, and to make some exchanges for sheep.

END OF THE FIRST VOLUME.

www.ingramcontent.com/pod-product-compliance
Lightning Source LLC
Chambersburg PA
CBHW051848300426
44117CB00006B/308